MW00685097

Single, Yet ❦ Not Alone

A Spiritual Guide for Latter-day Saint Singles

JAN MORGAN

Single, Yet Not Alone
Copyright © 2008 by Jan Morgan
All rights reserved

No part of this book may be reproduced in any form whatsoever, whether by graphic, visual, electronic, filming, microfilming, tape recording, or any other means, without the written permission of the author, except in the case of brief passages embodied in critical reviews and articles where the title, author, and ISBN accompany such a review or article.

Neither this book nor its author has any authority to speak for The Church of Jesus Christ of Latter-day Saints. The viewpoints and opinions expressed here are representative of the author. All stories are real but people's names and some situations have been changed to protect the identification of the contributors.

Published and Distributed by:

Anela Press
P.O. Box 1585
Fair Oaks, CA 95628
(916) 903-7299
Fax (916) 241-9906
Web site: anelapress.com
E-mail: anelapress@sbcglobal.net

Cover Design: Bookwrights Design
Editors: Sana Christian and Corinne Memmott

ISBN: 978-0-9818168-1-4
Library of Congress Control Number: 2008904797
First Printing June 2008
10 9 8 7 6 5 4 3 2 1
Printed in the United States of America

TABLE OF CONTENTS

INTRODUCTION

"THE TIME IS COMING when no man or woman will be able to stand on borrowed light. Each will have to be guided by the light within. If you do not have it, you will not stand."[1]

Singles in The Church of Jesus Christ of Latter-day Saints are among the first to experience what Heber C. Kimball predicted so long ago. As violence, crime, and environmental and social pressures rise in the world around us, our life circumstances become more difficult. Many of us struggle to make ends meet and shoulder the load of daily responsibilities on our own. For some, inner conflicts build in efforts to ward off feelings of loneliness, loss, ambiguity, and disappointment. Adding the increasing difficulty in these latter days to remain true to baptismal and temple covenants, and it is amazing any of us "hangs in there!"

Perhaps even more amazing is how many singles continue to participate in a "marriage and family-oriented" church. The world certainly does not support us in our dedication, nor do our natural drives encourage us to attend church—"the natural man is an enemy to God" (Mosiah 3:19). Merely attending church can prove a challenge as couples or families sit huddled together because, even when accepted, we are aware on some level of what is not around us. We notice the difference and can feel conspicuously single.

Many of us know all too well the feelings of the loss of a loved one either to death or divorce or of unfulfilled wishes or dreams. We know loneliness, the depths of which only those who have experienced it can fully understand. We know the struggle to endure, especially when life's path is not the one we expected. Some become independent out of necessity, only to crave some form of inter-dependency in our lives. Although such pressure is familiar to all, single or married, the intensity magnifies for singles because we often face these challenges and endure them alone.

So, with so many pulling at us to compromise and give up our values and faith, why don't we? What keeps us going to church—dedicated, or at least trying to be—even when it is a struggle?

I believe this is what Elder Kimball meant by "the light within." That light is our personal testimony of the Savior and of His love. It motivates us to seek an understanding of Him as well as a relationship with our Father in Heaven, and encourages us to remain faithful. Those who do not develop this inner strength either stay on the periphery of the Church or become inactive, for, without it, the pressures are just too great.

In this day and age, a single member's activity in the Church is a tribute to the light within, to their inner bond with God, and to their deep-rooted testimony or desire for such. We tolerate, handle, and eventually enjoy the differences encountered with others as we worship God and build a relationship with Him. Church becomes a wonderful place to worship, and the spiritual energy a tremendous resource and support. We grow beyond the

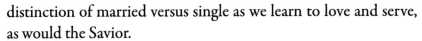

distinction of married versus single as we learn to love and serve, as would the Savior.

The light also helps us realize that, although the Church is family oriented, the basis of the gospel and applying its principles is oriented to each individual. Every ordinance but marriage is a one-on-one process. Even birth and death we experience alone.

Other people often help our understanding, awareness, and spiritual growth, but no one can be spiritually awakened for us, nor can we have a relationship with God through another. In our own hearts we feel the healing power of the atonement, come to know God through prayer, and hear and follow the inspiration of the Holy Ghost. These are very intimate and personal moments, and, ultimately, singular one-on-one experiences with God.

We also recognize that, although everyone has a different story to tell with different life circumstances, everyone has the same lessons to learn. It is as if we are climbing the same mountain, all on different sides, with no two journeys looking alike and every story different, from the tragic to the mundane. But those who keep climbing reach the same destination and learn the same life-lessons—faith, hope, reliance on God, and to grow and reach outside ourselves and love as the Savior loves.

We understand that each of us has a mission to fulfill here on earth. Some marry and devote their time and talents while raising families and others have the unique opportunity to share time and talents with people outside of a family of their own.

Marriage is necessary for exaltation and will occur for all who are faithful, if not in this life, then in the world to come. But what a tragedy it would be to spend our lives waiting for this one requirement while neglecting the development of others essential for exaltation such as faith, virtue, and charity. Our lives could very well be wasted if we allowed our singleness to keep us from blessing the lives of others and fulfilling our life's mission. Not only would we miss out on the joys of the present, but we would also miss the rewards of the eternities.

You who have weathered the tests, who have had your testimonies tried and yet continue to be faithful, what valiancy! Your understanding and awareness are priceless commodities to be shared with those who still struggle to understand the gospel and to live in harmony with the Spirit. You are essential in our Heavenly Father's plan. He needs those who are strong and righteous to carry His love to the world around us and to bring forth His kingdom.

To those who feel the struggle, who think the path is too rugged, too steep, and too treacherous, do not give up! Yours is the very trial that will create the strength within to help you to become the asset you really are. By enduring and growing beyond these challenges, you will develop the divine potential our Father in Heaven knows you have.

For some, this book will enlighten. For others, it will validate the path which you are presently taking. This book is for all singles—young or old, female or male, divorced, widowed, or never married. Pressures differ with each of us, and, as varied as are our backgrounds and circumstances, so also are our emotional, social, and physical needs. Nevertheless, we all have things in common because of the plan of our Father in Heaven.

Single, Yet Not Alone identifies those spiritual commonalties, and, more particularly, solutions that can work for all, regardless of marital status. It identifies those road markers along life's path that help us, as single members of the Church, with our journey and our efforts to continue to be faithful. It addresses gospel principles that can help us find peace and joy versus experiencing pain and anguish in life.

Remember the picture of the Savior in the Garden of Gethse-mane. It has been captioned, "I didn't say it would be easy. I only said it would be worth it." When we have our Father in Heaven, the Savior, and the influence of the Holy Ghost in our lives, we may be single, yet we are truly *not alone*.

Notes

1. Orson F. Whitney, *Life of Heber C. Kimball,* (1888 edition), 446.

Part One
YOU ARE NOT ALONE

Chapter One

SO, WHAT'S IT ALL ABOUT?

"IF THE SAVIOR WALKED INTO THIS ROOM this very moment, what would you do?" Jessie was caught off guard. Her eyes swelled with tears. Sitting next to her, I asked if she were okay with the speaker's question.

"If He were here," she whispered, "the lamb would lie down with the lion! Violence and abuse would end!" Her face lit up with joy as she expressed excitement at the very thought of His presence, "Oh, to bask in His presence and light!"

As Jessie shared her thoughts, I noticed the responses from the others in attendance. Most admitted they were unprepared to meet the Savior. Many felt a need to repent. Some felt fear. No one, except Jessie, felt prepared or even eager to see Christ.

I had known Jessie for a long time and knew she had been through tough times, was older, and living alone—just like me. Nevertheless, here in this moment, she was full of peace. Her countenance glowed as she talked about the Savior. Her eyes shone with joy and excitement.

As I listened, I wondered, *Why was Jessie's response so different? What did she know about the Savior that everyone else at the meeting seemed to miss? Why did she feel peace and joy rather than fear?*

I drove home from the meeting that night and contemplated the contrast between Jessie and the others, and then thought of my friend David.

David had joined the Church in his early twenties and taught Sunday School. He was handsome, charming, and longed for a family, wife, and children. During his final year of chiropractic school, I noticed him losing weight which he attributed to healthy eating. David's sense of humor began to fade and he offered explanations such as a visit with his family had not gone well or that he was under a lot of stress. Then, in a private state of weakness and overwhelmed in his efforts to cope with life, David resorted to a habit he had had before joining the Church. On a New Year's Eve, David overdosed on amphetamines and died.

The day I heard about David, I also received news about a beautiful, Latter-day Saint woman named Kathy. As a single mother of five and raising her children without financial support, she worked her way through school and had a successful position in the medical profession. However, exhausted, disillusioned, and overwhelmed, Kathy checked into a hospital for observation where she revealed her desire to die. She could not promise *not* to take her life.

What happened to David and Kathy? What was missing from their lives? Why did David regress so far that he took his life? What might save Kathy from the same fate?

As a licensed clinical social worker trained in psychotherapy, I could analyze their childhoods and the possible wounds to their psyche resulting from life experiences. As an unmarried single, I could empathize with their fears, loneliness and struggles. But then there was Jessie. She had experienced as rough or rougher "waters," and had found peace. How had she found peace when the world around her struggled for it? Is there a formula? Did she have a secret? Is there really a way?

Not Where We Thought Our Lives Would Be

Janet Lee, wife of the former President of Brigham Young University, tells the story about taking her five-year-old daughter, Stephanie, to register for kindergarten. When they reached the classroom door, there sat a teacher at a table with a box of crayons and paper. She asked Stephanie to choose her favorite color and write her name.

Stephanie looked at the box of crayons, but did not move.

The teacher asked again, "Stephanie, choose your favorite color, dear, and write your name on this piece of paper."

Janet's concern grew because she knew her daughter could spell everyone's name in her family. Nevertheless, Stephanie just stood there staring at the box of crayons.

Just as Janet was going to come to her daughter's aid, the teacher said, "That's okay. We will help you learn to write your name when you come to school in the fall."

On the way home, concerned that her daughter would be in the wrong class for her abilities, Janet asked her why she did not write her name.

"I couldn't," replied Stephanie. "The teacher said to choose my favorite color, and there wasn't a pink crayon in the box!"[1]

Often the "box of life" does not offer our favorite color of crayon. In some cases, we once had a favorite, but lost it. In other situations, our favorite color was abruptly smashed or destroyed. Some of us have changed our minds as to what is our favorite color, while others are still waiting for the right color of crayon to appear. Nonetheless, we are not where we expected ourselves to be in life. We wanted to be in the getting-married, happily married, or loving-family class, courses in which we are very qualified and fully capable of succeeding. Instead, we find ourselves among the widowed, divorced, childless, or not-yet-married, circumstances we never dreamed we would face.

Not knowing what lies ahead, some of us are content to go with the flow and willingly accept whatever unfolds. We trust all will work out in the end. However, for others, it is not that easy. Like Stephanie's mother, we are concerned, and we do not understand. We are afraid of what might or might not happen in the future. Not only do we not understand, but there seems to be a lot more required of us than what we originally thought would be the case. We did not sign up for this course—or did we?

Feelings of Inadequacy

Kimberly feels more and more alone as her friends and younger sister marry. She wonders what is wrong with her and fears she is being left behind. To make things worse, because of others' attempts to be kind, her sense of inadequacy increases when she is asked why she is not married or hears patronizing comments such as, "One day, you'll meet the right one," or "you'll be next."

Some singles believe we can not be valuable, contributing adults unless we have a family and a spouse. Sister Okasaki revealed how surprised she was when many members of the church expected her to resign from her calling as the first counselor in the General Relief Society presidency after her husband's death. She added that many assume singles "to be unhappy in their singleness."[2]

It is common to compare ourselves with others, especially when filled with self-doubt. Usually our analysis leaves us the lesser as we deny our own gifts and talents when others seem to have it all, or to at least have more. We can buy into the idea that we are not yet whole or complete, or worthy to serve or to offer what married people can. We wonder, *What do I have to share?* Meanwhile, waiting for the ideal time, we miss opportunities to give of ourselves when, if we give what we can, we might really make a difference.

Many of us build careers and feel good about our accomplishments. We fill our lives and keep ourselves busy, often out of necessity. Although we might accept and enjoy such independence, some of us may wonder if we are too independent. Did we out-do, over-do, or just plain not-do what was expected of us? As time goes by, we may wonder whether or not we should have been more accommodating, less dynamic, or even different than we are.

Denial and Fear

Some of us choose to avoid the fact that we are single. A man, recently widowed, described himself as "alone but not single." Actually, for those who married for time and eternity, but lose a spouse to death, a sweet assurance abides—knowing one day we will see that loved one again on the other side of the veil. What comfort that must bring.

For those divorced or not yet married, we may wonder who or what awaits us. Sometimes fear undermines our decision-making, and we compromise our values and goals, going places or involving ourselves in relationships that are spiritually and emotionally unhealthy. The worst thing we can do is to settle for something that is not genuine or good for us. Nevertheless, because we panic or are afraid to be on our own, we compromise.

Getting Off-Track

Making decisions without the counsel of another person who knows us and cares about our desires can lead to less than desirable outcomes. Unknowingly we start down a wrong path but if no one is there to notice or to give us the feedback which provides perspective, we can get off-track. For instance, we can end up experiencing a loss of self-esteem, become depressed, feel victimized, or turn to addiction. We may not realize how far we have strayed until, as in David's case, it is too late.

Fatigue

Melanie loved serving in the Relief Society presidency. Often, after a long day of work, she visited sisters in the Church. Many were young, full-time mothers who were overwhelmed by motherhood, struggles with their spouses, and depression. After these visits, Melanie would go home and sit alone with no children or husband, trying to find ways to replace what she had given emotionally that day. All she needed to re-energize herself was for someone to provide a hug, comfort, and reassurance that what she was doing was valuable.

Many of us press forward each day carrying a disproportionate share of responsibility, especially if we have children. Exhausted at the end of the day, we still need to run errands, keep the car fixed, shop for groceries, call the plumber, clean house, do laundry, read scriptures, and pray. Worn out, we wonder where we will get the energy to do the same things all over again the next day as we face life alone.

Resentment

Some of us resent our life situation and even blame God. Why would He allow this to happen? Isn't life supposed to get better, more meaningful, and happier over time? In some ways it does, but in other ways, it does not. We feel the emptiness within when we lose the person in our lives who seemed to make everything matter. We experience the ache in the pit of our stomach from the impact of another's negative actions upon our own lives. At times, the everyday struggles build up to be as powerful as the big blows, leaving us frozen, unable to move ahead.

We feel guilty for losing our tempers and becoming angry, for doubting God, for doubting ourselves. Our resentment and pain can become so deep we cannot see beyond them. To avoid these realizations we keep ourselves busy, but sometimes the unfairness of life does not make sense. We resent the feeling that we have been left behind especially when it seems everyone else's lives are progressing.

Loneliness

Many times, we have great support, but sometimes we do not. And, although we are expected to handle developments in our lives on our own, there are times when support would be so welcomed, just having a listening ear or for someone to show interest in our situation. When, at times, this does not happen, we can feel all the more alone and lonely.

Some of us enjoy our time alone as the solitude can bring much needed peace and quiet. We can get a lot of thinking done. We bask in the freedom to be whatever, however, whenever, or wherever we want. But there are times when life can be so devastatingly quiet, being all the more a reminder of what is *not* in our lives. Sundays and holidays can be the worst.

During these lonely moments, getting up in the morning can be a chore. Nights can seem so long and empty, so unbearable. These are the moments no one knows about, when we plead with God for comfort, searching for relief from the loneliness. We may even wonder if God has forsaken us. Our heart aches, and sometimes it seems better not to feel at all.

Finding Peace

Remember Jessie? The one who expressed excitement in seeing the Savior again and was at peace in her life? She had undergone fatigue, low self-esteem, confusion, fear, resentment, loneliness and had many struggles in her life, just like the rest of us. Her life was and is no different than yours or mine. And just like you and me, she will probably re-experience some of those same struggles in the future. But do you wonder how she found peace even in the midst of life's struggles? How she got beyond the pain to feel peace and joy?

Her story began in the mission field as a missionary. She told of how she communed daily with God through prayer. She said, "When I prayed, I felt as if He were right there talking to me, and I to Him. I knew His will, felt His Spirit, and was filled with His love and strength to do what He was asking me to do."

Years passed since her mission, and Jessie lost that connection simply due to life's distractions. She desired to renew her relationship with God and have the Spirit's influence back in her life. Knowing it was possible, because she once experienced it, she continued to pray. However, Jessie reported that life was "just too busy" and "so demanding" that she never took time to truly nurture her relationship with God and the Spirit. She later said, "Not doing so only made life more demanding."

Then one Labor Day weekend, she and four friends rode horses into the mountains of Yosemite National Park to camp at about 10,500 feet. Jessie left a world full of pressure and stress, longing for time in the wilderness to rejuvenate her soul. However, things did not go the way she expected.

As soon as camp was set up, a member of the group, a friend, began to make subtle, but very negative comments to Jessie. By evening, Jessie had had enough and commented to her friend about it in front of the others. Although her friend apologized in public, in private the negative comments persisted. The next morning, the comments continued. Jessie confronted her friend again, but this time a verbal explosion occurred between the two. Another group member also joined in against Jessie. (Note that

Jessie was already depleted and had gone on this trip to rejuvenate her soul.) Now after this contention, not only was Jessie upset, but she decided to pack her gear, leave the camp, hike down the mountain, and take a bus home.

Jessie wrote in her journal: "I was not more than half a mile from camp when I thought, 'Now, wait. I am in some of the most beautiful country in the world and I am going to go home and spend my holiday weekend alone, feeling stressed and depleted? I was too stubborn to turn back. But could I stay four days alone?" Jessie assessed what she had—three sandwich bags of trail mix, a bag of turkey jerky, and a cup of dry milk. But she had no tent. "Heavenly Father," she prayed, "will I be okay? Will you keep me safe?" She thought she felt a faint *You will be okay.*

Nature's Effects

Jessie hiked off the trail and found a secluded place beside a lake with a beach. Feeling safe, she decided to stay. She recorded, "It was impossible not to take in the freshness and calmness of the beauty around me. I was alone, yet there was a sense of refreshing freedom. I began to see, smell, and feel the absolute wonders of the mountains."

She continued, "I began to feel a change. The magnificence of the majestic mountains, some still snow-capped, and the purifying rays of the sun seemed to be softening my exterior shell of pride, selfishness, worldliness, and anger. Nature was tackling the natural man—woman—and how wonderful and welcoming was the siege. I felt free and alive, coming from a world so dead and draining. I praised God for this place, so straight from Him and so untouched by man."

Jessie spent the next two days alone, but enjoyed her stay because of the beauty of the mountains and the peacefulness she felt

while there. The third day, she reported, "I sat by the water, enjoyed its refreshment, and began to ponder and pray about life.
I felt my inadequacies before God—my pride, my sins, and my
stubbornness. I asked God to help me feel His spirit and love. I desired to commune with Him again. Although I felt the strength of
the mountains and their grandeur, I felt so many blocks between
God and myself. The funny thing was, every barrier was of my own
doing." Jessie was opening herself to the Spirit, and the Spirit was
having its effect on her.

That night Jessie ate dinner, and when the sun went down she
went to bed. She prayed, asking for protection, giving gratitude
to God for answering her prayers, and began a fast. "I needed to
reconnect with God like I remembered doing before but had not
done for so long. I felt a yearning to feel nearer to Him. I felt a
need to have questions answered and comfort given. It was worth
the sacrifice to fast and attempt to spend the day pleading for
God's grace and love."

Sunday was a day Jessie will never forget. As she washed up,
she spied a rock that sat on top of a hill overlooking a creek. She
climbed up on it and there she sat for hours, singing Church songs.
Then she said, "As I sang, I felt my pride melting away. I could not
contain the Spirit as it overwhelmed me. I cried tears of hope, tears
of joy, tears at feeling His mercy and His love. I felt His awareness
of me and His love for me. I felt His healing influence. The more I
felt His presence, the more I yearned for His loving care."

As she filled with His love, she continued, "I needed His guidance and His love. I needed Him back in my life. I hadn't realized
how empty I had become. Now, how easy it felt to feel His presence with no distractions than the beauty of the earth that filled
my soul. My heart was filled with gratitude and love."

Before ending her fast, Jessie went back to the rock above the water. "I stayed there passing answer after answer through my mind to the questions I offered in earnest prayer until I felt a reassurance from the Spirit which was the right answer to each question asked." She wanted to know what to do about the conflict with her friend. She wanted to know how to recreate her relationship with God and the Spirit. She wanted to know about her future regarding life and marriage.

She found an answer as to how to approach the conflict with her friend that was neither attacking nor blaming. She needed to apologize for confronting her friend in public and ask what she might have done to upset her. Jessie realized that in order to have the relationship she desired with God on a more permanent basis, she needed to rid herself of pride, selfishness, and the barrier of sin. Regarding her future, she felt impressed that someone wonderful was out there for her, but it would be a long while before he would come into her life.

She recorded, "The funny thing about all this is that after my prayer and day of fasting, I felt so connected to my Heavenly Father. No longer did it matter what or how far away marriage would be. Suddenly, there was meaning and contentment in my life. I no longer felt fear; nor did the pressures of the world seem to bother me. While in those mountains, although it seemed I had nothing, in reality I had everything. I experienced the effects of the Atonement of my Savior and had my Heavenly Father and the Holy Spirit back in my life. I was happy and filled."[3]

Jessie experienced nothing short of a mini-miracle. Her life was transformed as she removed the barriers that held back Heavenly Father's and the Savior's love. She realized the need to maintain those connections and do whatever necessary to keep our Father in Heaven, the Savior, and the Holy Spirit present in her life. In her efforts to commune with God, she not only experienced our

Heavenly Father's love but His acceptance of her. She realized His awareness of her needs and His ability to fill her emptiness with His love. She is at peace. Although she is single, she is truly *not alone*.

Notes

1. Janet G. Lee, "Choices and Challenges," *Ensign*, February 1995, 59.
2. Chieko Okasaki, (talk for singles delivered at Oakland Temple, summer 1997).
3. Jessie's Personal Writings, September 1996.

Chapter Two

Finding Peace

So, HOW DO WE GET BEYOND THE PAIN to feel peace and joy? How do we find the energy to accomplish all the tasks at hand and still feel good about ourselves and our lives? How do we move forward or overcome fear, particularly when suddenly alone? How do we fill the voids?

The answers lie in the gospel; however if we are too busy and "cannot see the forest for the trees" as goes the saying, our adversities can blind us to the solution offered by our Father in Heaven. Nonetheless, it is the very gospel principles that allow us to experience peace in the midst of hardship.

Consider the pioneers. Are our struggles really any different than theirs? Fortunately, we are not losing our lives and those of our family members as they did in their efforts to endure. However, I believe we face as great a challenge. Just as the pioneers battled against the elements for their physical life, we struggle against pressures in efforts to protect our spiritual and emotional life, the eternal consequences of which are far greater.

Most of us are on our own to overcome these struggles and we are often our own source of physical and emotional support. We find ways to cope, but can grow weary. Sometimes we get that desperate feeling inside and can be so caught in the moment that we cannot feel or recognize God's love. Our vision can become blurred.

We begin an endless search for what would make us feel better, or perhaps change our situations—something that will take away the pain or fill the emptiness. We search externally for happiness, constant pleasure, fame, even wealth, only to find life unsatisfying, lonely, disappointing, and disillusioning.

We chase after higher education, immerse ourselves in work, relationships, therapy, diets, drugs, food, or turn so far inward that we block out the world around us. This self-centeredness can turn to obsessions, depression, physical illness, and addictions. We are filled for a time, but that familiar emptiness returns and our yearning continues.

We try using our intellect and willpower, but neither fills the void. We spend our lives striving to prove we can do it alone—resisting any notion that we are weak, "We don't need anyone's help."

Eventually, in our weariness, when things are extremely bad, we become aware that we need something greater than ourselves or anything in this world to fill the emptiness. What relief when we realize there truly is something greater! At this point we are not too proud to ask for help. We are ready to "look to God and live" (Alma 37:47).

We Need God

"I would that ye should come unto Christ, who is the Holy One of Israel, and partake of his salvation, and the power of his redemption" (Omni 1:26).

The Savior said, "Come unto me, all ye that labour and are heavy laden, and I will give you rest. Take my yoke upon you, and learn of me…and ye shall find rest unto your souls. For my yoke is easy, and my burden is light" (Matthew 11:28–30).

The Savior continues: "Behold, I stand at the door, and knock: if any man hear my voice, and open the door, I will come in to him" (Revelation 3:20). He is there, just waiting to "come in" if we but open the door. He invites us all to follow him—what love! Yet, He will not force any one of us to follow. What agency—freedom to choose. We must make the choice to open the door of our heart and invite Him into our lives. No one can do that for us.

Sammy remembers his first year away at BYU. He was beset with loneliness and overwhelmed by life's problems. Far away from family and friends, he needed comfort, advice, and counsel. He called his parents. No one answered the phone. He called his close friends back home, one by one. No one answered. Frantically, he tried calling everyone he could think of. Not one was available to answer his call.

He could have felt sorry for himself or made the moment traumatic. Instead, Sammy hung up the phone, got down on his knees, and began to pray. As he shared his concerns and fears with God, he realized his greatest concern was feeling alone and lonely. He desired closeness with someone he cared about and who cared for him.

After his prayer, Sammy felt impressed to open the scriptures. He opened to Doctrine and Covenants, 93:45. There he found "I will call you friends, for you are my friends." He felt comfort knowing that no matter who is or is not around, God is always there.

The Savior not only atoned for us and is the mediator between our Father in Heaven and us, but He can also be—and will be—our truest friend. He is there anytime, anywhere, no matter the circumstances. When we decide to follow Him, He encircles us with His love. It is His love that makes the journey possible, even when the pathway gets rough. But, you ask, how do we make that happen? How can we truly bring Him into our lives to feel His peace and experience such joy?

Needing A Sure Foundation

The Savior said, "I am the way, the truth, and the life. No man cometh unto the Father, but by me" (John 14:6). When we are humble enough, we realize there is no way we can successfully make it through life without Christ. The Savior gives us a wonderful example of relying on Him in the following parable:

"Therefore whosoever heareth these sayings of mine, and doeth them, I will liken him unto a wise man, which built his house upon a rock: and the rain descended, and the floods came, and the winds blew, and beat upon that house; and it fell not: for it was founded upon a rock. And every one that heareth these sayings of mine, and doeth them not, shall be likened unto a foolish man, which built his house upon the sand: and the rain descended, and the floods came, and the winds blew, and beat upon that house; and it fell: and great was the fall of it" (Matthew 7:24–27).

When we build our house on sand, without any sure foundation, our house can fall with the slightest breeze. Just as in life, if we have no sure foundation, our sense of self and well-being are based on temporary things that are fleeting. If we have a disappointing relationship, someone offends us, or life becomes too stressful, we can crumble. On the other hand, if we build our house on rock, our foundation is based on something grounded, sure, and greater than ourselves. We become less vulnerable to outside forces. No matter the circumstances, we remain steadfast.

Only by building on the rock of Jesus Christ can we weather any storm. "Remember that it is upon the rock of our Redeemer, who is Christ, the son of God, that ye must build your foundation; that when the devil shall send forth his mighty winds...it shall have no power over you...because of the rock upon which ye are built" (Helaman 5:12).

A short time after his wife's death to cancer Elder Richard G. Scott shared in general conference: "True enduring happiness with the accompanying strength, courage, and capacity to overcome the most challenging difficulties comes from a life centered in Jesus Christ. Obedience to His teaching provides a sure foundation upon which to build. That takes effort. There is no guarantee of overnight results, but there is absolute assurance that, in the Lord's time, solutions will come, peace will prevail, and emptiness will be filled."[1]

Obedience to the Savior's teachings and applying the basic principles of the gospel—faith, repentance, baptism, and the gift of the Holy Ghost—help us dig deep to find that all-important rock for our foundation. These basic principles start us on the path toward truth and help us remain steadfast, but most critically, they lead us to Christ. We need not just faith, but faith in Christ; not just repentance, but repentance to remove any barrier that stands between God and ourselves. We need baptism to covenant and commit to follow the Savior no matter what, and the Holy Ghost's guidance in our efforts to stay firmly on the path.

Sometimes we think nothing should ever go wrong once we build upon the rock of our Savior. We are surprised when life's destructive storms continue to strike and we may even think we are being destroyed. We can feel betrayed because we thought we did our part to build the house on rock. The foundation still stands yet now the house is gone or so it seems.

Perhaps God saw a huge crack down the middle of the house and knew it needed repair. If we surrender to His will, He will fix the crack, not just by patching it and leaving risk for future default, but by restructuring the whole house. Knowing there is a strong foundation, restructuring is possible, and the needed home can be built.

C. S. Lewis describes that process. "Imagine yourself as a living house. God comes in to rebuild that house. At first, perhaps, you can understand what He is doing. He is getting the drains right and stopping the leaks in the roof and so on: you knew that those jobs needed doing and so you are not surprised. But presently He starts knocking the house about in a way that hurts abominably and does not seem to make sense. What on Earth is He up to? The explanation is that He is building quite a different house from the one you thought of.... You thought you were going to be made into a decent little cottage: but He is building a palace. He intends to come and live in it Himself."[2]

As painful and self-sacrificing an experience such as restructuring your house can be, we usually do not understand and appreciate how important the process is until it is done. This is the way to wholeness and joy, even when the storm is raging around us. And when the restructuring is complete, not only are we humbled by the process itself, but by the realization of the profound change and fulfillment it brings into our lives.

But It Gets Really Tough

Often when we are taken to our limits, we may want to give up and say, "Forget it." The reality is, at some point, we are going to be tried and tested. Expect it. And when you are surprised by your reaction to the situation, realize you are reacting the way any other human would, given the same situation. We are human, as much as we hate to admit it.

This can be very discouraging. However, when we realize there is a purpose for such moments—to be taken beyond our limits, where we get stuck and have difficulty handling it—understanding the purpose becomes very encouraging. "Truth sets you free" (John 8:32).

Also, understand that despite the tough moments in life, ultimately we are to experience joy. Lehi told his son Jacob that "men are that they might have joy" (2 Nephi 2:25). Joseph Smith also taught us, "Happiness is the object and design of our existence."[3] So how do we discover joy in the midst of tough times?

Imagine someone betrays you, hurts you, destroys a dream, ruins your reputation, or in other words, snatches the emotional rug from under your feet. The betrayal and hurt are deep. It will likely take more than what you have inside to move beyond the pain, anger, and disappointment. The Lord asks you to love this person and forgive (see Matthew 18:21). However, what if the betrayal and hurt are so deep you are unable to let go, to forgive, to love this person? You are commanded to forgive and love (see Matthew 5:44). But how can you do this?

God does not want you to live in denial of the wrong done to you nor pretend everything is okay and make it look good on the outside. He does not mean for you to ignore abuse and not take care of yourself or to stay in a harmful situation. You must acknowledge what has happened and do what you are prompted to do. Even then, we are asked to forgive, and to love—even when others justify our anger, and we are encouraged to talk badly about the person. In our minds, they deserve revenge. However, God says, "Vengeance is mine." Here is the chance to replace evil with good (see Romans 12:19, 21) and to love, not to pretend to love, but to genuinely love (see Matthew 5:44).

If we have the Spirit in our lives, we can probably take care of small offenses on our own. But sooner or later along comes the larger crisis such as that of death, divorce, betrayal, or some form of deep hurt. No matter how hard you try, you cannot release the anger, resentment, or emotional pain. Where do you get help?

Nephi felt the struggle, "…why should my heart weep and my soul linger in the valley of sorrow, and my flesh waste away, and my strength slacken, because of mine afflictions?…that the evil one [may] have place in my heart to destroy my peace and afflict my soul? Why am I angry because of mine enemy?" (2 Nephi 4:26–27).

Acknowledging and expressing the grief related to his afflictions and the anger he felt because of his enemies, Nephi says: "Awake my soul.… Rejoice, O my heart, and give place no more for the enemy of my soul" (2 Nephi 4:28).

Anger is a terrible enemy of our soul and can destroy our peace as it did with Nephi. In fact, anger can do more damage than the original wound inflicted by the offender. It can make us bitter, harden our hearts, and take away our humility. However, Nephi says to "rejoice." In other words, be happy.

So how do we let it go and do what Nephi does to "awake" and allow no place for the enemies of our soul? How do we get to a point of being able to rejoice? Compounding this situation we can also become upset with God for His seeming negligence in not only allowing but in not easing our pain. How long before we succumb to bitterness and anger?

This is where most of us get stuck. We want to counsel God. We want Him to rescue us, and take away the test or trial. However, we are warned about counseling God. "Seek not to counsel the Lord, but to take counsel from His hand" (Jacob 4:10).

It is possible to rid ourselves of the enemies of our souls such as anger, hurt, and fear, and to love and forgive, no matter the situation, as God asks. We can feel peace and joy, even in the midst of life storms. We can do this by making a change within ourselves. A change of heart, a change in our souls, can only occur through the Atonement of Christ.

Notes

1. Richard G. Scott, "Trust in the Lord," *Ensign*, November 1995, 17.

2. C. S. Lewis, *Mere Christianity,* 1996, 176—copyright © C.S. Lewis Pte. Ltd. 1942, 1943, 1944, 1952.

3. *Joseph Smith History,* 2nd ed., vol. 5, 134–135.

Chapter Three

THE ATONEMENT OF CHRIST

HAVE YOU EVER NOTICED that when you perfect one area of your life and then start working on another, the area you thought you had perfected often ends up no longer perfect?

We, by ourselves, will never reach absolute perfection. We will never be the perfect parent, the perfect worker, or the perfect friend. In fact, it is not supposed to happen in this life. We *will* make mistakes.

The reality is we are human, and, as such, imperfect. Remember the "natural man is an enemy to God" (Mosiah 3:19). Peter states that all "have sinned, and come short of the glory of God" (Romans 3:23). But the Lord tells us, "Be ye therefore perfect" (Matthew 5:48). How can we be perfect if we are by nature imperfect? Why the dichotomy—we being imperfect, yet commanded to be perfect?

It may help to consider that the Greek translation of the word "perfect" from the King James Version of the Bible means, "whole, fully developed, mature, or complete." So, when the Savior said, "Be ye therefore perfect," the Greek translation yields, "Be ye therefore whole, fully developed, complete."

Imagine you dropped a precious vase and broke it into several pieces. Even with your best glue job, you cannot fix the vase to make it perfectly whole again. When we feel broken and our life is in pieces, all we have to do is give those pieces over to God. Through His healing power, He mends what we cannot mend for ourselves. What once was broken, He restores to make it whole—perfect, as if there had been no break.

The Savior tells us "the whole need no physician, but they that are sick" (Mark 2:17). Paul says, "Jesus Christ maketh thee whole" (Acts 9:34). The scriptures go on to give us an example of wholeness, "little children are whole," (Moroni 8:8). That is probably why the Savior continuously reminds us to "become as little children" (Matthew 18:3).

The basics of the gospel—faith, repentance, baptism, and the gift of the Holy Ghost—support our spiritual foundation. These are essential to our spiritual growth and fill our cup half way. However, the process of truly taking the Savior at His word and allowing Him into our lives adds what we cannot and fills the cup. Actually, we are very egotistical if we think we can reach perfection or wholeness on our own.

"Nevertheless, the Lord God showeth us our weakness that we may know that it is by his grace, and his great condescensions unto the children of men, that we have power to do these things" (Jacob 4:7).

The only way we can be "perfect," complete or whole is through Jesus Christ, by relying on Him. In fact, life was planned this way. Heavenly Father knew we would need the Savior—to use repentance and His grace to make up for what we cannot do.

Moroni clarifies this: "Yea, come unto Christ, and be perfected in him … that by his grace ye may be perfect in Christ; and if by the grace of God ye are perfect in Christ, ye can in nowise deny the power of God" (Moroni 10:32).

We reach perfection only through the power and grace of the Savior.

Taken to the Limits

I personally came to understand the meaning of peace and feeling "whole" as a result of a difficult experience in my life. I had moved to California and planned to begin my graduate studies program. Since I needed money for tuition, I decided to invest in a real estate project. I had previously been a real estate agent, but had discovered that buying homes and renovating them for resale was much more lucrative. As the California real estate market was unfamiliar to me, I was a bit intimidated by the idea of buying a house on my own. So I asked a good friend to partner with me and he agreed.

The market was at its peak and we decided it made more financial sense to build a house for resale. I would manage the business part of the project. My partner assured me he knew construction and agreed to oversee the building of the house from the ground up—something I had never done before. I would help him and he would help me. My partner estimated six months to complete the project. I figured nine. We began the project, but unfortunately things did not go as planned.

My partner rarely showed up on the job site to perform the work as promised. Initially, I talked nicely to him about the problem. Later I nagged, then begged, and finally, resorted to yelling, all to no avail. It seemed no matter what I did, he would not honor our agreement. I became increasingly frustrated and angry.

Every penny and extra minute of time I had went into this

project. Graduate school loomed. I had orchestrated the project to make it profitable and manageable for the budget we set and for the market at the time. Had it happened on schedule, we would have realized a substantial profit. Two years later, the project was still unfinished, but could be sold. My partner refused to sell, subsequently not paying any profit to me.

Suddenly, I was left with no money to pay living expenses. The pressures of attending graduate school and getting this project completed became overwhelming. My partner talked badly about me to family and friends attempting to defame my character and portray me as a bad Mormon. I must admit, I did not help the situation with my obvious anger and high level of frustration fueled by sheer exhaustion from trying every way I knew to resolve our situation.

I had never experienced such emotional upset, nor expressed such strong reactions. How could this person, a former friend, not only betray me, but have no consideration for the sacrifices and contributions I had made to this project?

I was beyond my ability to cope and hated this person for the hardship he had created. He had lied, deceived, and taken financial advantage of me. However, I could not continue to carry the anger and stress without the effects ruining my health. How was I going to get beyond the extremely resentful and angry feelings?

One night, enraged, full of tears, my heart pounding, I felt like I was going to explode. I knelt down, even with all the fury inside me and said, "God, I cannot handle this. This one is way beyond my ability to cope. I am going to go crazy with anger and stress if I do not get some kind of relief."

While praying, I pictured myself giving this whole situation over to God and said, "I will focus on keeping Thy commandments and following the Spirit for direction and help."

A change occurred, but not with the circumstances. In fact, it took another three years and thousands of dollars before the business issue was settled. Nevertheless, that night I found something far greater than the money lost on this project. Never had I been in such a deep state of anger and resentment. Never had I been so betrayed and misrepresented to others so unkindly. And most important, never before had I so needed to solely rely on God for His mercy and strength.

However, as Alma expressed, nothing was "so exquisite and sweet as was my joy" and peace when I let go and let God take charge (Alma 36:21). To my amazement, every resentment left, every angry feeling was gone, and the course I needed to take was clear. I was now able to do what was necessary to terminate this project, free of the crippling anger toward my partner. Even though I did not like what my partner had done, and do not plan to do business with him again, I could love him. Now that is victory!

No amount of money can equal the lesson I learned that when we turn over to God what we cannot handle and then focus on living His word and following the Spirit, no matter the circumstances, peace and joy can exist in our world.

Incorporating the Atonement

Many are familiar with, and sometimes refer to, the word "atonement" as "at-one-ment." "At-one-ment" implies a reuniting with God, even when we are in our separated state from God, here on earth. The Atonement takes an imperfect being like ourselves and, when united (at-one-ment) with a perfect being, even Jesus Christ, we, by His wholeness, become whole. His perfection makes up for the disparity.

Just as the Atonement, if we use it, compensates for the difference between perfection and us as sinners, so too it is with any emotion we cannot get beyond. "Surely he hath borne our grief, and carried our sorrow...[was] wounded for our transgressions...was bruised for our iniquities: the chastisement of our peace was upon him, and with his stripes we are healed" (Isaiah 53:4–5).

The Savior sacrificed Himself—taking every sin and every pain in this world upon His shoulders—so we would not have to carry that burden if we but give our sin and pain to Him. We give Him our anger, hurt, sorrow, loneliness, disappointment, and loss; and He fills us with His love so we can move beyond those feelings. What we cannot do or handle, He completes. He will, if we let Him, make up for our shortcomings.

We say, "God, I cannot handle this feeling anymore. I cannot get beyond it without Thy help. I need Thee to take this burden and pain." Then picture in your mind giving the whole situation, the hurt, resentment, loneliness, and confusion to Him. Promise Him you will focus on keeping the commandments, listen to and follow the Spirit, and accept His will, whatever the outcome. As you do, you will find your burden lightens because now all you need to do is follow His guidance and focus on keeping the commandments. The Savior, through the atonement, takes care of the rest.

We can trust Christ at His word when He says He "will take upon him the pains, sins, and the sicknesses of his people" (Alma 7:11). He will carry the burden. There is no sin or pain too great or too small that He will not take, if we willingly turn it over to Him. He said, "Have ye any that...are afflicted in any manner? Bring them hither and I will heal them...for I see that your faith is sufficient that I should heal you. And...he did heal them every one" (3 Nephi 17:7–9).

How reassuring to know the Atonement can relieve us of any ailment or pain or shortcoming we have. We give the Savior our shortcomings, He gives us the ability to overcome and grow beyond them. Because of Him we develop more character, more understanding, more patience, and become more like God.

The Savior invites us all to take advantage of this wonderful opportunity availed by the Atonement and be whole. All we have to do is to invite Him into our lives, trust what He says is true, then give to Him what we alone cannot do.

Chapter Four

KNOWING JESUS CHRIST

So, HOW CAN WE TAKE THE SAVIOR AT HIS WORD and truly believe Him if we have no sense of who He is? How can we trust someone we do not know?

The Savior said, "This is life eternal, that they might know thee the only true God, and Jesus Christ, whom thou hast sent" (John 17:3). Notice the word "might" is used. It does not say once we are baptized, we will know God. It is not a guarantee that once we keep the commandments we will "know" Him. As we do what He asks, we gain a testimony of the commandments (see John 7:17) and a testimony of Him, but to truly know God and His Son Jesus Christ takes more than just that doing.

Remember the story the Savior tells of those who came wanting to enter into the kingdom of heaven? Remember what they said? "Didn't we prophesy in your name...and in your name do many wonderful works?" Remember what the Savior said to these people? He said, "Ye never knew me; depart from me" (Joseph Smith Translation, Matthew 7:33).

"But wait! I was a Relief Society president, bishop, elders quorum president. I did my home teaching. I deserve something." And most likely, these people will get something very nice. However, for those who "know" God, He recognizes and allows in. To those who never come to know Him, He says "Ye never knew me; depart from me."

It could be said when it comes to getting into heaven, it's not *what* you know but *who* you know that counts.

The Interview

Many of us say we know the Savior, but how many of us truly know Him? If He were to walk into this room, would we recognize Him? We can live the law and do the acts of prayer, fasting, obeying commandments, and going to church, but does this represent having full knowledge?

I am reminded of the classic story about three men being interviewed to enter heaven. The interviewer asked the first man as he entered the room to tell him what he knew about the Savior. The man told all of the details of the Savior's birth in a manger, of Christ's life and of His death. The interviewer asked if he could add anything else. The man thought for a moment, adding nothing. The interviewer thanked him and escorted him out of the room.

The second man entered the room, and the interviewer asked him to tell what he knew about the Savior. This man recounted the life of the Savior, emphasizing the Atonement and the meaning it had in his life—to repent. The interviewer asked if there were anything more he could add. The man said He was the literal Son of God and bore his testimony of knowing the Savior lives today. The interviewer thanked him and led him out of the room.

As the third man entered the room, he looked at the interviewer, fell to his knees, and cried, "My Lord, My God."

It is one thing to know the gospel and know "about" the Savior. It is a totally different thing to truly know Him.

Many Church members are absorbed with the "do's" and the "don'ts." Many are clear about required tasks, such as raising children, serving in the Church, and fulfilling life's responsibilities. We are very busy! However; we must be careful not to get so caught up in our responsibilities and practices in the Church or in our life situations that we miss the very core of the gospel—as the Savior taught, developing a sincere and deep relationship with Him that rejuvenates, refreshes, fulfills, and makes whole.

Let us look at ways to develop such a relationship and what it looks and feels like once we incorporate the Savior into our lives.

Feast Upon the Words of Christ

The Savior teaches us about Him and the way to become like Him through scripture. "Feast upon the words of Christ; for behold, the words of Christ will tell you all things what ye should do" (2 Nephi 32:3). He admonishes us to "search the Scriptures...which testify of me" and "ponder upon the things which I have said" (John 5:39; 3 Nephi 17:3). And when we are confused as to the next step to take in our lives, Psalms reminds us that the words of Christ are "a lamp unto [our] feet, and a light unto [our] path" (Psalms 119:105).

If we do not yet know Jesus, what He is like, and what He would do, we can turn to the scriptures and learn about Him— not only by His counsel and commandments, but by His life and His example. Step-by-step, piece-by-piece, as we study His teachings and His life, then pray and ponder the scriptures to personalize the meaning and message they have for us, our perspective increases, and we gain a greater understanding of our Lord, Jesus Christ.

What Would Jesus Do?

As we study the words of Christ and His life, we must apply His words in our lives, incorporate His teachings into our every day activities, and do what we commit to each week when we take the sacrament—to "always remember him" (Moroni 4:3).

We must ask ourselves, "What would Jesus do?"—not just on Sundays and when it feels good to do so, but in any and every situation in which we find ourselves. "What manner of men [women] ought ye to be? Verily I say unto you, even as I am" (3 Nephi 27:27).

As we align our actions with His and live according to His will, we become more like Him. We become Christlike. As we become more like Christ in every situation, we come to know what He experienced, what He felt, and why He did what He did for us. Most importantly, we come to know Him.

I am convinced if each one of us took the time to find out what the Savior would do in each and every situation in our lives, we would no longer need therapists and social workers. There would be no more abuse or misuse of each other. This relates to every marriage, every parent-child relationship, and every human relationship we encounter.

Experiencing the Savior's Love

Becoming like the Savior in action alone is still not enough to truly know Him and have His companionship in our lives. We must experience Christ deep in our heart, with every fiber of our souls, and feel the cleansing and healing power that only the Savior can give—to feel the renewal to life being "born again" implies.

Alma asks, "Have ye spiritually been born of God? Have ye received his image in your countenances? Have ye experienced this mighty change in your heart…and felt to sing the song of redeeming love?" He adds, "…can ye feel so now?" (Alma 5:14, 26). In

other words, have you felt His personal love for you and that deep
sense of peace that only His spirit brings? Have you felt as if your
heart were on fire and felt the pain melt away? Have you felt to
share His love with the whole world and with all of His creations?
Moreover, if you have in the past, can you feel so right now?

This happens when we are "spiritually...born of God." We
experience the Savior's all-consuming love, His all-consuming acceptance, and His all-consuming light in our lives. Have you ever
known anyone who adored you so much that in his or her eyes you
could do no wrong? An aunt, a baby-sitter, a teacher, or a grand-
mother? Or have you ever held a young child in your arms toward
whom you felt total love and adoration?

This is merely a hint of what the Savior's love is like—a personal, absolute adoration for each one of us. Even if we were the
only one here on Earth, He still would have given His life, because
He so loves each and every one of us and wants for us the joy and
eternal rewards His sacrifice brings. His love is greater than any
love we can ever imagine or find here on Earth, and is far more
filling, refreshing, and sweet.

As a teenager, Sandy remembers craving to know more about
Jesus. She read everything she could—the Book of Mormon, the
Bible, even the book, *Jesus the Christ,* to better understand Him.
However, it never seemed to quench her thirst. Then one day at
girls' camp, she went to gather wood. Alone and away from the
mainstream of camp, Sandy suddenly felt embraced by an overwhelming love that seemed to touch every part of her being. She
dropped the wood and began to cry over the warmth and power
that love she felt created within her.

Years later, troubled by adversity in life, a single mother of two
infants, and having nightmares of war and death, she prayed to
God for relief from these nightly intrusions. One night, in another

dream, she saw hundreds of people coming over a ridge in the horizon. Running from what she thought were her attackers, she saw in the center of the on-coming crowd a small light. She stopped to look at the light, and as it came closer, she saw in it a figure she knew to be the Savior. The same love that overwhelmed her as a young girl was suddenly present in her dream. Standing still, as she soaked up the light and love, she said to herself, "Who am I that He would come to me?" In her heart, she hoped He would come to her, and in her dream, He did.

Although a dream, Sandy felt the Savior's total adoration and love for her. She felt His calming, all-consuming love and acceptance. She explains that since her dream, she has felt that same light and love in her life. Moreover, she adds, "Just as one can tell the difference between the scent of broccoli and apple pie or cookies when baking, as we feel His love, we recognize it, we know it, as we do a familiar aroma."

We knew the Savior's love long before we came to this earth when we dwelt with Him and our Eternal Father in Heaven in the premortal existence. As we desire to have His love in our lives, having a sincere heart and real intent, and living in tune with the Spirit, we will experience His all-familiar love even while here on earth.

Having a Change in Heart

As we open ourselves to that love, we begin experiencing what Alma meant when he asked if we have experienced a "mighty change in [our] hearts" (Alma 5:14). You see, the Savior's love is all-consuming, hence our hearts and minds go through a natural change. As we allow it to affect us, our whole soul, person, and persona change, and we take on a more Christlike character.

We put off the "natural man," and we begin "putting on Christ." We give up the old, that of our limited, narrow-minded, self-centered self, and take on the new—that of having the mind of Christ, becoming Christ-centered, and receiving "his image in [our] countenances" (Alma 5:14).

No longer do we desire evil or to do harm, to hurt, or to seek revenge. In fact, no longer is that even a part of us, as our hearts are changed. No longer do others offend us, nor does our anger last, because our hearts are filled with His love and peace.

We shed fear, anxiety, greed, and the need to control because we trust God. In addition, because we are full of love and aware of His presence in our lives, we feel whole. We do not feel alone, nor *are* we alone.

Have you ever noticed someone who has the image of God in his or her countenance? They have a pureness and realness not seen in others. Their eyes have a sparkle that demonstrates a sense of joy and peace even when things are not perfect. The world can crumble around them, but the peace and comfort they feel in their hearts does not shift. These trials somehow end up as stepping-stones and help make them who and what they are today.

Those who have His image in their countenances become instruments in God's hands to help support and lift others. The Savior explains, "I am the vine, ye are the branches: He that abideth in me, and I in him, the same bringeth forth much fruit: for without me ye can do nothing" (John 15:5). It is as if they take themselves out of the way and let God take over and literally become instruments in His hands. These people become extensions, branches, and partners with God by extending His love. No longer is it a duty nor is it an attempt to be like the Savior, but rather He has become part of them and it becomes a privilege to serve no matter the circumstances.

Christlike Character in a Concentration Camp

An amazing story of Christlike behavior under extreme circumstances in our modern day is told in a story Kitty de Ruyter tells of her mother when she, her six siblings, and mother were in a Japanese concentration camp in Indonesia during World War II. Sister de Ruyter shared this story at a Brigham Young University (BYU) singles conference, June 1996.[1]

The family had lived in Samara Java, Indonesia, then known as the Dutch East Indies, for it was owned by Holland at that time. They were an educated and wealthy family. When Germany invaded Holland on May 10, 1940, the Japanese landed in Indonesia. Kitty's father—an officer in the Indonesian army and a Japanese prisoner who escaped captivity and led efforts against his captors—was considered a "marked man" by the Japanese.

To find Kitty's father, the Japanese placed Kitty's mother and children under house arrest. When Kitty's father learned this, he surrendered to the Japanese, hoping to save his family from harm. However, early one morning the Japanese took the family to concentration camps, anyway—Kitty's mother and the girls going one way, the boys another.

The women lived in barracks infested with flies, rats, and lice. There were long lines to the toilet. They slept on a dirt floor. Kitty recalls each morning her mother offered a prayer to thank Heavenly Father for their lives, food, and water. She also prayed for Kitty's brothers and dad.

Their mother continually reminded her daughters, "Love your enemies, bless them that curse you, do good to them that hate you, and pray for them that despitefully use you, and persecute you" (Matthew 5:44). She told the girls, "to waste your energy on hate would be a total loss, because hate consumes your energy needlessly and will get you nowhere. But love," she said, "will build your character and enhance it."

One day, Kitty's mother was assigned the task of selecting twenty-eight women, from ages twelve to twenty-two, to be used as prostitutes for the Japanese officers. She prayerfully took this problem to the Lord. Not knowing whom to choose or how to follow through with such a task, she devised a plan to shave off all the hair of some sixty young women of that age group.

When the officers came for the young women, they were, said Kitty, "repulsed and treated the act as an open revolt." Blaming Kitty's mother, they stripped off her clothes and humiliated her in public.

One officer asked how she could have done such wrong, defying her orders. He made the mistake of putting a blow-horn to her mother's mouth, through which she said, "My God has sanctified some things in our lives, and virtue is one of them....We will protect our virtue at all cost, even unto death."

The enraged Japanese officer then bound the mother's arms over her head, tethered her to a pole, and beat her. The officer cut a cross on her back with his sword, then continued beating her with a belt and its buckle, catching and ripping out pieces of flesh.

She did not scream, but Kitty remembers tears streaming down her mother's face. When they cut her loose, she fell down to the ground. As she tried to get up, they kicked her down. Then they sentenced her to two weeks in "the pit."

"The pit" was a hole in the ground, about six feet deep, with standing or squatting room only. The top was covered with chicken wire. Usually no one survived this punishment due to the emotional, psychological, and physical trauma.

When Kitty's mother was led to solitary confinement, she turned to her children, reminding them to "remember the Garden of Gethsemane." She asked her children to wait and pray for her, as the Savior had asked His closest comrades to wait and pray for Him in His most agonizing moments.

Kitty's mother survived the pit. When released, the other

women cleaned her with water they had saved and picked out the maggots nesting in her rotting back. Once clean, she fell to her knees to thank Heavenly Father for preserving her life. She believed God had given her a miracle, for it had rained three times while she was incarcerated. She had been able to collect fresh water by pushing dirt up against the wall to keep it from her filth. And she had learned how to catch the food thrown to her with her mouth.

The same afternoon of her release, Kitty and her mother were in line for food. Kitty, seeing her mother in such great pain and hearing her moaning while in line, got angry. Full of hatred, she threw her cup of water into the face of a Japanese officer. She spat on him, and shouted some very unkind remarks.

The officer drew his sword. Kitty froze—certain her hands would be cut off. Her mother, already in great pain and with much difficulty, placed her hand on the sword. She begged her daughter to pick up the cup and apologize. Kitty could not move. The mother picked up the cup, bowed to the officer, as required, and apologized for her daughter. She explained her daughter was still young and had not developed the discipline necessary to master her emotions, and to please have mercy on her child. She added that if punishment needed to be given, she, the mother, would take the punishment.

Kitty's mother was a remarkable example of someone who had already sacrificed herself for the virtue of all the women in the camp. Now she was willing to take the punishment for her daughter when she, the mother, had already been tortured beyond what most could survive. But a miracle then happened. The officer placed his sword into its sheaf, took the cup and filled it with water. He offered it to the mother with both hands, a sign of respect, and said. "It is I who needs to apologize to you for not recognizing the majesty of your womanhood."

"Truly you have the spirit of Ishido in you," responded the mother. (Ishido is a warrior of wisdom, and this was a great compliment to the Japanese soldier.) He then turned and walked away, leaving the women alone.

This compelling display of Christlike character by a brave mother, even in the most horrifying of times, demonstrates the power of being true to God and living life as would the Savior. Truly, she knew God in a way that gave her the strength to be an instrument for Him even through the midst of incredible suffering.

Coming to Know Jesus

Many members of the Martin and Willie handcart companies came to know Christ in their efforts to cross the plains and settle the Salt Lake Valley. Everyone in the company felt impressed to make the trek despite not knowing what would lie ahead. Many suffered tremendous adversity and bore great sorrow and pain from the cold and elements along the way. Many even lost their lives.

In 1856, Francis Webster, a member of the Martin handcart company, wrote about his experience in his journal. "I have pulled my handcart when I was so weak and weary from illness and lack of food that I could hardly put one foot ahead of the other. I have looked ahead and seen a patch of sand or hill slope, and I have said I can go only that far and there I must give up, for I cannot pull the load through it.... I have gone on to that sand, and when I reached it, the cart began pushing me. I have looked back many times to see who was pushing my cart, but my eyes saw no one. I knew then that the angels of God were there. The price we paid to become acquainted with God was a privilege to pay."[2]

Both Kitty's mother and Francis Webster are like the man who sold all he had for the "pearl of great price" which was likened to the kingdom of God (Matthew 13:46). They displayed a tremendous amount of love, devotion, and understanding of their God, to serve, love, and follow even amidst suffering. They chose not to focus on pain but on the privilege to be loyal and one in character with our Father in Heaven and our Savior Jesus Christ.

To be like Christ, we must experience, to some degree, what He experienced. How else would we develop a greater level of compassion and understanding? When we feel as He feels, love as He loves, remain loyal as He remained loyal to our Father in Heaven—no matter what the circumstances, even if on a cross—we begin to truly know, not just about Him, but truly come to *know* the Savior of the world.

Faith in Christ

Some of us are still at the point where we hope what we are saying is true, never mind trying to develop enough faith to become valiant. So how do we develop the hope and faith to even begin to have the character exemplified by Kitty's mother and those of the Martin and Willie handcart companies?

Alma gives a wonderful discourse on this. He says, "But behold, if ye will awake and arouse your faculties, even to an experiment upon my words, and exercise a particle of faith, yea, even if ye can no more than desire to believe, let this desire work in you" (Alma 32:27).

Alma is saying if we merely have a desire to know the Savior and feel His love, the first thing we do is plant that desire in our hearts. Okay? So…let's apply his challenge right here and now! Do you want to know the Savior and feel His love in your life? Do you want to know that all-consuming love and acceptance? And if you have felt it in the past, do you desire to feel it again? Allow yourself to *want* to feel Jesus' personal love and attention. We all have to start somewhere, so let's start by planting that desire.

"Now we will compare the word unto a seed. Now if ye give place, that a seed [even a desire] may be planted in your heart, behold, if it be a true seed, or a good seed, if ye do not cast it out by your unbelief… it will begin to swell within your breasts; and when you feel these swelling motions, ye will begin to say within yourselves—It must needs be that this is a good seed, or that the word is good, for it beginneth to enlarge my soul; yea, it beginneth to enlighten my understanding, yea, it beginneth to be delicious to me" (Alma 32:28).

Once you have planted the seed, take time to *nourish* it through study and prayer. Your desire to feel Christ's love will begin to enlighten and enlarge your soul. As you continue to nurture this seed, desire will grow into faith and faith into action. Your understanding, with time, will become knowledge, and you will experience the Savior's love and influence in your life.

Alma's approach to building faith reminds me of the mother who told her young son to clean his room. The room was a mess. This little boy, like most children, looked at the room and felt overwhelmed. The results? Nothing was cleaned. Later, the mother said, "Let's clean your room. You make the bed, and come back and tell me when you have it done." The little boy made the bed. When he told her, she praised him for his work and then said, "Now pick up all the Legos off the floor, no other toys, just Legos, and I will time you." He went running to get the task done. With less effort in the long run, step-by-step, the room was cleaned, and everyone felt good.

Sometimes, when we look at the enormity of a job, we are overwhelmed and feel like we will never be able to complete the task. However, Alma, wise like the little boy's mother, breaks the process down into steps. Step one, plant the *desire* within. Step two, begin *nurturing* that desire. Step three, *continue to nurture* that desire.

And behold, as the tree beginneth to grow, ye will say: Let us nourish it with great care, that it may get root, that it may grow up, and bring forth fruit unto us. And now behold, if ye nourish it with much care, it will get root, and grow up, and bring forth fruit.

But if ye neglect the tree…behold it will not get any root; and when the heat of the sun cometh and scorcheth it, because it hath no root, it withers away.…

Now, this is not because the seed was not good, neither is it because the fruit thereof would not be desirable; but it is because your ground is barren, and ye will not nourish the tree, therefore ye cannot have the fruit thereof.…

But if ye will nourish the word, yea, nourish the tree as it beginneth to grow, by your faith with great diligence, and with patience, looking forward to the fruit thereof, it shall take root; and behold it shall be a tree springing up unto everlasting life. [Alma 32:37–41]

As we continue to nurture our desire to know Christ using study, prayer and fasting, we will want to conform to the Savior's teachings and apply His atoning sacrifice in our lives. The depth of our commitment deepens as we realize our worth as children of God, and begin experiencing the very fruit Alma promises.

"And because of your diligence and your faith and your patience with the word in nourishing it,…behold, by and by ye shall pluck the fruit thereof, which is most precious, which is sweet above all that is sweet, and which is white above all that is white, yea, and pure above all that is pure; and ye shall feast upon this fruit even until ye are filled, that ye hunger not, neither shall ye thirst" (Alma 32: 42).

This fruit is the personal love of Jesus—He who loves you so much that He would lay down His life and die for you. In fact, that is exactly what He did!

The Savior desires to bless each one of us with His love and healing power. He is just waiting for us to open up to His love by planting the seed, asking in prayer, and taking the steps Alma suggests. As we do, Jesus will be there for us, and we will come to know and experience His love and adoration in our lives. Even in a world full of pressure and stress, we can feel His peace. "Peace I leave with you, my peace I give unto you; not as the world giveth, give I unto you" (John 14:27).

Notes

1. Audiotape by Kitty de Ruyter—"As I Have Loved You," (Covenant, 1989).

2. William R. Palmer, "Pioneers of Southern Utah," *The Instructor,* 79 (May 1944), 217–218, as quoted in *Generations of Websters,* Amy L. Van Cott and Allen W. Leigh, Thomas Webster Family Organization, Cedar City, Utah, 1960, 61–62.

Chapter Five

KNOWING HEAVENLY FATHER

WHEN YOU PRAY, TO WHOM DO YOU PRAY? When the Savior prayed, to whom did He pray? He did not pray to Himself. He prayed to His Father—our Father in Heaven. Beginning the great intercessory prayer, John tells us, "These words spake Jesus, and lifted up his eyes to heaven, and said, Father, the hour is come; glorify thy Son, that thy Son also may glorify thee" (John 17:1).

The Savior prayed to God concerning His Apostles and those who followed them: "Neither pray I for these alone, but for them also which shall believe on me through their word" (John 17:20–21).

In the Garden of Gethsemane, Christ pleaded with God, "And he went a little further, and fell on his face, and prayed, saying, O my Father, if it be possible, let this cup pass from me: nevertheless not as I will, but as thou wilt" (Matthew 26:39).

The Savior taught us how to pray when he said, "After this manner therefore pray ye." He then gave us an example, the Lord's

Prayer (Matthew 6:9) and showed us to whom we pray when He started His prayer with, "Our Father which art in heaven"—not just His Father but "Our Father" who is in heaven.

As we kneel in prayer, we pray in the name of the Savior, but we talk directly to the source, the very God, Elohim, Himself. Could our Father in Heaven be more personal and loving than to offer such a gift, to talk directly with Him—all we have to do is pray and we have our Father in Heaven's attention?

Joseph Smith clarifies this point: "It is the first principle of the gospel to know for a certainty the character of God, and to know that we may converse with Him as one man converses with another."[1]

President Gordon B. Hinckley gave testimony of our Father in Heaven: "I look to Him as my strength. I pray to Him for wisdom beyond my own. I seek to love Him with all my heart, might, mind, and strength. His wisdom is greater than the wisdom of all men. His power is greater than the power of nature, for He is the Creator Omnipotent. His love is greater than the love of any other, for His love encompasses all of His children, and it is His work and His glory to bring to pass the immortality and eternal life of His sons and daughters of all generations (Moses 1:39)."[2]

The scriptures are filled with examples of the power of prayer. Enos prayed for forgiveness and received a remission of his sins. Alma prayed that his son would be called to repentance. An angel visited Alma's son and his life was changed. Joseph Smith prayed and received a personal visit from our Father in Heaven and the Savior.

Although we may not receive as dramatic a response from prayer, we can rest assured our sincere prayers will be heard. And if we are in tune with the Spirit and listening intently, we will receive the answers we seek. "Whatsoever thing ye shall ask the Father in my name, which is good, in faith believing that ye shall receive, behold, it shall be done unto you" (Moroni 7:26).

Personal Revelation

I have heard it said prayer is our way to talk with God and personal revelation is God's way to talk with us. Personal revelation is the way our Heavenly Father communicates with us. "I will tell you in your mind and in your heart by the Holy Ghost.... This is the spirit of revelation" (D&C 8:2–3).

Often, we get on our knees, say a prayer, then jump right up, and go about our daily tasks—cheating ourselves out of one of the most important components of prayer. If we open our hearts to God, share our joys and sorrows, ask our questions, share our concerns, then end our prayers by being still—pondering in our minds and hearts those things presented to Him—inspiration will come. If we pray and then listen, inspiration will come. Furthermore, as we follow its direction, we will be able to discern between our thoughts and the Spirit's promptings.

The important point is to wait for some kind of inspiration before getting off your knees from prayer. Then follow through with the inspiration you receive. Often nothing that unusual happens and we may wonder if God is testing our obedience. Then at other times truth is revealed and promptings are given which may not make sense at the moment but which lead to the very things that need to happen in the end.

In the mission field we were working hard but no one seemed interested in our gospel message. I felt discouraged and as though I were not fulfilling a very good mission. I remember asking God in prayer what was missing. After praying for help, I heard in my mind a quiet, yet clear, comment, "Just love them." "What?" I said to myself. "I eat their food and drink their water. I sleep in their housing and struggle to speak their language. How can I love them more?"

As the day wore on, I contemplated what I had heard. Obviously, I was not "loving" enough. Did I even know how to love—truly love? Then the thought came to me, *Put yourself in their shoes.*

A few days later we were teaching a family, and, for the first time as a missionary, I could feel what life must be like for the father whom we were teaching—the joys as well as the pain. My heart went out to him as I bore testimony of the truthfulness of those things we were sharing.

Two weeks later, that man and his family joined the Church. Because of their example, another family joined the Church. Suddenly, baptisms were coming "out of the woodwork." Weeks later, a young "greenie" (a new missionary) asked, "Sister Morgan, how do you do it? How do you get so many baptisms?" At first I was surprised. Then I realized he was right. We were having many baptisms. It did not take long to tell him the secret of our success. I said, "Ask God. He will tell you what you need to know and do." Then I added, "Just love them."

This was a powerful moment in my life. I not only gained a deeper understanding of the power of prayer, but, just as important, how powerful are the answers that do come when we willingly listen and follow those promptings. I am grateful for such a lesson on love and for the knowledge that when we pray with sincere hearts, with real intent, we can receive answers to our prayers through personal revelation.

A One-to-One Relationship

The interesting thing about personal revelation is that it is personal—a one-to-one communication. God will inspire you about that which is important for you. That is why it is personal—no one else receives revelation for you, or you for them. What great insight and comfort to know we can be guided by a source that is all-knowing and all-powerful.

Shayla needed understanding and guidance as she struggled in her marriage. Initially, she felt good about marrying Barry, but now he was not living up to his marriage covenants and had become emotionally and physically abusive. Both Shayla's bishop and stake president had advised her to leave her husband, but Shayla loved Barry and wanted to help him. However, she was acutely aware of the potential danger she and her children faced. She needed to know for herself the right thing to do. Therefore, Shayla made a decision, and, as she prayed about it, she felt a warmth come over her and a complete peace. "Yes, you need to go and go soon" was her impression. Knowing God had given her an answer, she packed her bags and those of her children and left, never regretting her decision.

How wonderful it is to know our Father in Heaven speaks with us through personal revelation if we will listen, not just during times of special need but each and every day of our lives. Just thinking about this ought to make each one of us feel valued and loved because the answers to prayer which we receive are very personal, private, and specific for each one of us.

As singles, we have a wonderful opportunity to build this one-to-one relationship with our Heavenly Father. He is our source, our partner—particularly during times when we are by ourselves. When we build a relationship with Him and develop our ability to receive personal revelation, we will have "ears to hear" (Luke 8:8) and eyes to see far beyond what would be ours on our own.

We Can Know the Truth of All Things

We are also promised that if we pray with real intent and a sincere heart, we can know the truthfulness of all things (see James

10:4–5). Joseph Smith took this promise to heart when he knelt in the grove of trees, asking God which church was true. He received a revelation that would change the world. We, too, can take the challenge to know the truthfulness of all those things that matter in our own lives and are beneficial for us to know.

We must not take this lightly. It has been said we cannot expect a million dollar answer for a five-cent prayer. To commune with God takes effort, time, desire, real intent, and a pure heart. We may need to fast, ponder, study, and follow the Spirit. However, if we are sincere, humble, and faithful, we can be assured we will receive guidance and direction. It may not be what we want or how we expect an answer to come, and the answers may not make sense in the short run. Nevertheless, with faith, putting those impressions into actions, we will feel God's presence and know His will in our lives.

Nephi, confronting his brothers when they wanted understanding of the words their father spoke, asked if they had inquired of God. They said they had not. He reminded them, "Do ye not remember the things which the Lord hath said? If ye will not harden your hearts, and ask in faith, believing that ye shall receive, with diligence in keeping [His] commandments, surely these things shall be made known unto you" (1 Nephi 15:11). Nephi's brothers were just not willing to take the time or make the effort.

How do these answers come? Sometimes they are unspoken words in our minds, a flash of an idea, or a feeling in our hearts. Answers can come as impressions to do or not to do something. It has been known and recorded in scripture that our Heavenly Father talks with us in dreams and, in some cases, by visitation. Many times a person is sent into our lives to teach or to help us. Often we are given experiences from which we learn meaningful lessons. As we soften our hearts to the Spirit, we will see when and how answers come.

How Often Should We Pray?

Almulek, teaching the Zoramites, said:

Cry unto him when ye are in your fields, yea, over all your flocks. Cry unto him in your houses, yea, over all your household, both morning, mid-day, and evening. Yea, cry unto him against the power of your enemies. Yea, cry unto him against the devil, who is an enemy to all righteousness. Cry unto him over the crops of your fields, that ye may prosper in them.... But this is not all; ye must pour out your souls in your closets, and your secret places, and in your wilderness. Yea, and when you do not cry unto the Lord, let your hearts be full, drawn out in prayer unto him continually for your welfare, and also for the welfare of those who are around you. [Alma 34: 20–27]

Nephi told his people to "...pray always, and not faint; that ye must not perform any thing unto the Lord save in the first place ye shall pray unto the Father in the name of Christ" (2 Nephi 32:9). Alma adds, "Pray continually... and thus be led by the Holy Spirit" (Alma 13:28).

We need our Heavenly Father in our lives daily and especially when facing major decisions involving, for instance, employment, raising children, where to live, and in our relationships. He desires to bless us: "Pray always, and I will pour out my Spirit upon you, and great shall be your blessing" (D&C 19:38). In addition, because Heavenly Father knows all, from the beginning to the end, His understanding and counsel will not fail us. "Counsel with the Lord in all thy doings, and He will direct thee for good" (Alma 37:37).

So when we experience troubles in our lives, first ask, "How often do I pray?" and "How involved am I when I pray?" Because when the lines of communication are "down" with our Father in Heaven, we can lose focus, and those things that separate us from God arise more quickly. Remember, "Pray always, lest ye enter into temptation" (D&C 31:12).

If we continually pray and receive no answer, we then must look at what might be blocking that personal revelation. We can be assured the obstruction is not from God. The barrier may be within us—our pride, sin, or fear. Whatever it is, removing the obstacle opens the way to personal inspiration.

The Love of God

Knowing our Father in Heaven means we have, at some point, felt His all-consuming, life-changing love. It means we have taken the time, made the sacrifice, and cleansed our souls, which allows His light and love to enter. There is nothing sweeter or more fulfilling than His love for us (see Nephi 8:11-12).

However, if we place the world's perception of conditional acceptance on our Father in Heaven, we will likely focus on God's justice and miss His loving mercy. Our training in this life with conditional love may keep us in a cycle of constantly working to win God's love by actions. But God's love is not conditional. He loves us no matter what we do or don't do, if we sin or are "bad," or if we ignore and deny Him (see Romans 8:35–39). Our actions determine what eternal rewards await us, not whether or not God loves us. His love is always there, unconditionally. It is the nature of God for He *is* love (see 1 John 4:8).

No one on this earth loves us more than our Eternal Father in Heaven. And once we experience His love, we are never the same, for we understand our divine value and begin accepting others and ourselves as He does as valuable individuals who matter. We realize we are literally His spiritual offspring—sons and daughters of God—and the closer we grow to Him, the clearer becomes this knowledge and understanding. Psalms 82:6 reads, "Ye are gods; and all of you are children of the most High." And, "The Spirit itself beareth witness with our spirit, that we are the children of God" (Romans 8:16–17).

We can experience our Father in Heaven's love in our lives as we open ourselves to our Father in Heaven in prayer. President Spencer W. Kimball talked about feeling God's love through prayer, "Sometimes feelings press upon us. A spirit of calmness assures us that all will be well. But always, if we have been honest and earnest, we will experience a good feeling—a feeling of warmth for our Father in Heaven and a sense of His love for us. It has sorrowed me that some of us have not learned the meaning of that calm, spiritual warmth, for it is a witness to us that our prayers have been heard. And since our Father in Heaven loves us with more love than we have even for ourselves, it means that we can trust in His goodness, we can trust in Him; it means that if we continue praying and living as we should, our Father's hand will guide and bless us."[3]

Comfort and healing await those who willingly commune with our Father in Heaven through prayer. As we build a relationship with Him, we will feel as if He is right there with us, as if His arms are holding and comforting us and letting us know He loves us. When we pray we can feel as if we are kneeling before His feet seeking comfort and forgiveness. And when we are in need of a blessing, we can feel as if His hands are blessing us.

As we purge from our lives those things which stand in the way of His Spirit, we will feel our Father in Heaven's love. His love is all-consuming. "Wherefore, my beloved..., pray unto the Father with all the energy of heart, that ye may be filled with this love" (Moroni 7:28).

When blessed to have a loving father in this life, we easily comprehend what it is like to have a loving Father in Heaven. For those whose fathers were not so loving here on earth, it may be more difficult to understand that we have a Heavenly Father who does love us.

If you have not had a loving father in this life, the wonderful news is that a father's love is available for you now. Right now. God, your Heavenly Father, will help you learn what it is like to have Him, a loving Father, in your life. He will help you shed the fears that keep you from experiencing His love and truly knowing Him and feeling His arms around you. Comfort, love, and a softening heart await as you trust and begin building, through prayer and personal revelation, that relationship with Him.

Could any other knowledge be more powerful—to know that we are truly divine by nature, sons and daughter of a living God who loves and adores us? We are spiritual beings merely having a mortal experience while on earth.

On those days when you feel overwhelmed and need someone to talk with, try talking with God. Build a lasting relationship with Him by pouring out your heart and asking for the blessings you need. Then "be still, listen, and know that [He is] God" (Psalm 46:10).

God Is Our Father

What words of comfort come from the hymn "O My Father":

O my father, thou that dwellest in the high and glorious place,
When shall I regain thy presence and again behold they face?
In thy holy habitation, Did my spirit once reside?
In my first primeval childhood, Was I nurtured near thy side?

For a wise and glorious purpose Thou hast placed me here on
    earth,
And withheld the recollection of my former friends and birth;

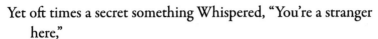

Yet oft times a secret something Whispered, "You're a stranger
  here,"
And I felt that I had wandered from a more exalted sphere.

When I leave this frail existence, When I lay this mortal by,
Father, Mother, may I meet you, in your royal courts on high?
Then, at length, when I've completed all you sent me forth to
  do,
With your mutual approbation Let me come and dwell with
  you.[4]

No greater love awaits us, no greater peace and joy, no greater
sense of our true, eternal nature is felt than that which is ours when
we experience our Eternal Father's love in our lives.

Notes

1. *History of the Church of Jesus Christ of Latter-day Saints*, 2nd ed, rev.,
ed. B. H. Roberts, 6:305.

2. Gordon B. Hinckley, "The Father, Son, and Holy Ghost," *Ensign*, November 1986, 49–50.

3. Spencer W. Kimball, "First Presidency Message 'Pray Always'," *Ensign*,
October 1981, 5.

4. "O My Father," *Hymns,* no. 292.

Chapter Six

KNOWING THE HOLY GHOST

WHEN THE SAVIOR LEFT THIS WORLD, He gave us a gift so we would not be alone. He gave us the Holy Ghost. "But when the Comforter is come, whom I will send unto you from the Father, even the Spirit of truth, which proceedeth from the Father, he shall testify of me" (John 15:26). We are told that "the love of God is shed abroad in our hearts by the Holy Ghost which is given unto us" (Romans 5:3–6).

President James E. Faust describes the Holy Ghost: "The Spirit of the Holy Ghost is the greatest guarantor of inward peace in our unstable world.... It will calm nerves; it will breathe peace to our souls.... It can enhance our natural senses so that we can see more clearly, hear more keenly, and remember what we should remember. It is a way of maximizing our happiness."[1]

The Savior knew He would not be with us in person, so He gave us a companion to teach, guide, comfort, heal, and do all those things the Savior would do if He were here. The presence of the Holy Ghost is a wonderful and magnificent gift and its presence ensures that we are truly not alone.

As members of the Church, we receive a confirmation blessing right after baptism which bestows the "gift of the Holy Ghost." This gift blesses us with the constant companionship of the Holy Ghost. "The Holy Ghost shall be thy constant companion" (D&C 121:46). This means not just having moments with the Spirit, but having its constant companionship in our lives as we live in tune with the Spirit.

Now this entails great responsibility because having the Spirit's constant influence in our lives requires living worthily, "the gift of the Holy Ghost…cannot be received through the medium of any other principle than the principle of righteousness, for if these principles are not complied with, it is of no use, but withdraws."[2]

When we exercise faith in the Savior "the Holy Ghost" will "…have place in [our] hearts" (Moroni 7:32). In other words, we cannot expect to have the companionship of the Holy Ghost when we do not believe and accept those whom this Spirit represents. In the absence of faith, manifestations of the Spirit are forfeited. As we seek to be like Christ and try to live the principles of righteousness, the Holy Ghost will be a constant companion to guide and direct us.

Is it not amazing the resources our Father in Heaven has given to help us through life? We have the power of the Atonement of Jesus Christ, the power of prayer as we commune with God Himself, and the gift of the Holy Ghost as a constant guide and influence, moment-by-moment, day-by-day, year-by-year. Access to these divine resources is such a wonderful gift and provides us comfort, guidance, and inspiration.

Let us look at the many ways the Spirit can impact us, and how to implement its companionship in our lives.

The Holy Ghost Reveals Truth

As mentioned earlier, our Father in Heaven uses the Holy Ghost to provide us with inspiration and revelation. Alma, telling the people of his day how he knew the teachings of truth, said, "I say unto you they are made known unto me by the Holy Spirit of God. Behold, I have fasted and prayed many days that I might know these things of myself. And now I do know of myself that they are true; for the Lord God hath made them manifest unto me by his Holy Spirit; and this is the spirit of revelation which is in me" (Alma 5:46).

Nephi, wanting understanding of his father's teachings said, "After I, Nephi, having heard all the words of my father, ... which he spake by the power of the Holy Ghost ..., I ... was desirous also that I might see, and hear, and know of these things, by the power of the Holy Ghost, which is the gift of God unto all those who diligently seek him" (1 Nephi 10:17).

All over the world, missionaries invite investigators to seek truth through the power of the Holy Ghost by sharing Moroni's promise: "And when ye shall receive these things, I would exhort you that ye would ask God, the Eternal Father, in the name of Christ, if these things are not true; and if ye shall ask with a sincere heart, with real intent, having faith in Christ, he will manifest the truth of it unto you, by the power of the Holy Ghost. And by the power of the Holy Ghost ye may know the truth of all things" (Moroni 10:4–5).

Sometimes we have difficulty seeing the simplicity of the truth before us. Brigham Young, one of the most profound and prolific leaders of our time, stated, "When I saw a man without eloquence, or talents for public speaking, who could only say, 'I know, by the power of the Holy Ghost, that the Book of Mormon is true, that Joseph Smith is a Prophet of the Lord,' the Holy Ghost proceeding from that individual illuminated my understanding, and light, glory, and immortality were before me."[3]

Those who are filled with the Spirit will recognize the Spirit bearing testimony of truth no matter the lack of eloquence of the delivery. "He that receiveth the word by the Spirit of truth receiveth it as it is preached by the Spirit of truth....Wherefore, he that preacheth and he that receiveth, understand one another, and both are edified and rejoice together" (D&C 50:21–22).

Now the "truth of all things" is not limited to gospel truths alone. The Holy Ghost manifests truths in all areas of our lives, as I learned while attending graduate school to become a clinical social worker. Taught by some of the most talented professors in the country, the plethora of information was outstanding. As we students attempted to build the theoretical foundation that would guide and direct our clinical interventions, many of my colleagues shifted their own theoretical base as quickly as a new theorist was introduced, seemingly to be more and more confused with each approach reviewed. Many questioned their own mental functioning and would identify with each new mental disorder as we came upon it in our studies.

Fortunately, I was not confused and learning was much easier for me when I included the Spirit into the learning process. I studied all the theories for the exams, but used only that which was confirmed by the Spirit in building the theoretical base that ultimately influenced my clinical practice.

The Holy Ghost shines a beacon of light in a world shaded by human philosophies and confusion. The gospel gives us a foundation of truth on which to build, and the Spirit helps add truth to that foundation, even in fields of science and research. The Holy Ghost confirms truth from error every step of the way if we cultivate its companionship in our lives.

The Holy Ghost Is a Guide

As we keep our lives in tune with the Spirit, it will guide and warn us when we need protection. Below, Jessica's story illustrates the importance of listening as well as following the Spirit.

Devastated when a long-term relationship ended, Jessica felt lonely and did not feel good about herself. Tim, who was in the elder's quorum presidency in her singles ward, asked her out, and after a few dates wanted to develop a more serious relationship. Jessica recalls having a feeling that she should not get involved. However, she enjoyed his company. He liked everything she liked and was full of personality.

Logically, dating Tim made sense and in her heart Jessica enjoyed his attention and companionship. After a while, Tim asked Jessica to marry him. Confused, she sought counsel from her bishop who encouraged the marriage. She said yes, but soon felt depressed, sad, and frustrated. She lacked enthusiasm to pursue the wedding plans.

One summer morning, working in her backyard, Jessica asked God what she should do. The message was clear, "Listen to your feelings." She thought, *I am sad and depressed, frustrated, and angry.* Despite what seemed to make sense, Jessica called off the engagement and ended the relationship.

The wisdom of her decision became apparent when Tim's true nature revealed itself. He became obsessed with Jessica, stalking her from behind bushes when she started to date again, sneaking into her house when she was away. It ended only after he came over one night, unable to handle his obsession, and for two and a half hours, verbally and physically abused her.

Jessica was grateful for having followed the Spirit not to marry this person. Nevertheless, how unfortunate it was that she did not listen to her original prompting and became seriously involved with him in the first place. She rationalized her decision with feelings and logic, overriding that deep level impression—the Spirit's promptings.

Three years later Jessica started dating Rick, not a member of the church. Again, she had an impression she should not get involved. But, again, she rationalized by saying he was a long-time friend, he made her feel good about herself, he was fun, and everyone liked him. Besides, she felt disappointment from dating Church members due to the earlier experience.

After a few months of dating, he also asked Jessica to marry him. Feeling happy and content with all his attention and affection, without seeking a confirmation in prayer, she said yes. Later, the very night he had proposed, while drinking and intoxicated, Rick date raped Jessica.

Now in my office, with these two horrible incidents in her life, what a tragedy it was when she said, "How easily it could all have been avoided had I only listened to and then followed those initial promptings."

Just like Jessica, many of us rely on what makes sense and what we think is best when making major decisions. Some of us react from our emotions and rely on just our hearts. Although both need consideration, in the end we must set our thinking and feelings aside and seek the Spirit's influence by connecting to that deep, underlying, in-your-soul feeling—not to what you want or what you think others want for you, but to that deep-down inner sense of what is good and right.

As we connect with the whisperings of the Spirit and follow them—even when the decision goes against logic or emotions, or both—the Spirit's influence will grow stronger in our lives, preventing us from being steered wrong. In fact, at times we will be amazed at the outcome of those decisions.

Jessica was in tune enough to hear and know what the Spirit was saying, but, unfortunately, she did not grasp the significance of following what she heard. Logic seemed to make more sense and feelings got in the way. Had she followed the promptings she received, she could have avoided the extra time and energy it will now take to heal and rebuild the fragmented pieces of her emotional self. "Enter in by the way, and receive the Holy Ghost, [for] it will show unto you all things what ye should do" (2 Nephi 32:5).

Promptings of the Holy Ghost

The Spirit also prompts us to help others. Its still, small voice can be as simple as the prompting an older gentleman received while on his evening walk, to take a different route than usual. Following this impression, he came upon a crying boy who had fallen from his bike and needed help with a loose chain and misaligned seat. The man fixed the child's bike, and as the boy rode off—with tears still shining on his face but now sporting a smile—he turned and said, "Thanks."

Listening to the Spirit may be life saving as in the case of a mother who felt impressed to stop her vacuuming and run directly to her neighbor's backyard, finding her 18-month-old, alone, about to jump in their pool for a "swim." When we listen and follow the Spirit, "by small means the Lord can bring about great things" (1 Nephi 16:29).

The Spirit lets us know—even at the very moment—when to turn away from an activity or action. Wise individuals will follow because they have learned that when we do not heed His promptings, the Spirit leaves and we are left on our own to make what, at times, can be very critical decisions. When we remember the "natural man is an enemy to God," without the Spirit's influence in our life, our natural drives can lead us toward spiritual destruction. Thus, when left alone to fight adversity, without the Spirit's influence, adversity can easily triumph.

Our relationship with the Spirit is vital, especially as we singles meet and date new people and make critical decisions in our lives. The Spirit knows. It represents God who is all-knowing. As we develop a relationship with the Spirit, keep its influence in our lives, know when it is communicating with us, and then use faith to follow its promptings, we will be guided even when life does not make sense. Its continual influence will let us know good from evil and help us avoid sore trials. What a powerful resource and blessing we have!

The Holy Ghost Sanctifies

Another benefit of the Spirit is Its sanctifying power. The scriptures tell us through "yielding [our] hearts unto God" comes sanctification. Helaman details how this happens: "fast and pray oft,...wax stronger...in...humility, and firmer...in the faith of Christ, unto the filling [of our] souls with joy and consolation, yea, even to the purifying and the sanctification of [our] hearts" (Helaman 3:35).

Each time we yield our hearts to God—through fasting, repentance, baptism, worthy participation in temple ceremonies, humble personal prayer, spiritual moments, or having faith in Christ—sanctification occurs. Darkness dissolves as the Spirit's light begins to take its place. The old gives way to the new, and we become more enlightened, more calm, more in love with life, and filled with greater love for God and others. As we continually yield our hearts to God, our humility deepens, and like fresh air to a wound, healing occurs.

The righteous develop that extra light in their countenances, that extra glow, by taking the time to submit to the influence of the Spirit, and allow its sanctifying process to purify their souls on a daily basis.

This is the process by which we prepare to one day be in the presence of our Father in Heaven, for "no unclean thing can dwell with God" (1 Nephi 10:21). As we live with the Spirit's constant companionship in our lives, we experience its purifying power.

The Holy Ghost Comforts

For some, the most effective impact of the Spirit is its comforting power. In our times of need, we can kneel and pray and ask for comfort. Our Heavenly Father will send us "the Comforter which is the Holy Ghost" (John 14:26).

The Holy Spirit is like a warm, soothing blanket on a cold, wintry night. The cold does not necessarily go away, but the warmth and comfort of the blanket help protect us from the effects of the harsh weather.

Carla knows the Spirit's comforting power. After a phone call from her sister informing her that her mother had cancer and would soon die, Carla cried uncontrollably. Faced with the imminent loss of her mother, Carla questioned *why cancer?* Her mother had lived a good, clean life. Carla was older, had not married, and needed her mother to stay here on earth!

Carla fell to her knees, her eyes full of tears, her heart full of emotion, asking to understand. Even though her mother would not live, Carla received something greater than understanding— reassurance that all would be well because Heavenly Father was aware and knew of the situation. When her mother passed away a few weeks later, Carla felt the calmness and peace the Spirit provides, knowing all was part of God's plan.

The Spirit gives comfort, not only by its still small voice but by the blanket of comfort draped around us. Like Carla, we may not know the purpose of our trials until the next life. But if we keep in tune with and follow the Spirit's direction, we will be blessed not only with reassurance of what is right, but also with the peaceable comfort provided by the Holy Ghost.

The Holy Ghost Enhances

With the Spirit's influence we become more than our natural selves. Hank is a good example. One morning, under pressure to get to work and get his four kids ready for school on time, his youngest son, four-year-old Jeremy, became demanding, clingy, and crying for Hank's attention. Hank felt his anger and impatience building, and told Jeremy to go to his room and stay there until he stopped crying. However, Jeremy refused and became more demanding.

Though ready to yell at Jeremy, Hank felt impressed to be nice and talk kindly with his son. Taking a deep breath, Hank knelt down to Jeremy's height, put his arms around Jeremy, and, while talking softly, discovered that Jeremy felt sad because he missed his "mommy" who had died six months earlier from cancer. As Jeremy shared his feelings and Hank provided comfort and assurance, within minutes Jeremy was able to finish getting ready.

Through the influence and promptings of the Spirit, Hank experienced a precious moment in his son's life as the Spirit helped him be what his son needed, someone with whom to share his grief. Not only did Hank learn a better way to solve a potentially disastrous problem, but at that needed moment, he became more than his natural self.

Elder Asay tells us, "Mortal men and women are endowed with marvelous abilities and potential. But however great these mortal powers may be, they are only a shadow of those powers that can be claimed through a linkage with the Holy Ghost."[4]

Our Father in Heaven tells us that He will not give a commandment nor allow any trial or life situation for us, while we are on this earth, that we cannot handle (see 1 Nephi 3:7). However, the key in meeting and overcoming difficult situations requires the Spirit's influence. In fact, if struggling alone, a situation may overcome us. With the Spirit in our lives, we are better able to face our challenge so that we become the conquerors and grow closer to our divine potentials.

Elder L. Tom Perry discusses his observations of the power of the Holy Ghost in the lives of his fellow General Authorities. "I have watched my brethren, strengthened by the Holy Ghost as their constant companion, shoulder enormous workloads at an age when most men would be confined to rocking chairs. They are subjected to strenuous travel schedules but remain undeterred as they enthusiastically engage in building the kingdom of God. Recently the realization came to me that the great spirit that attends my brethren, helping them magnify their assignments, is available to all the members of the Church. Everyone who earnestly seeks the Holy Ghost can be lifted and guided. As Elder James E. Talmage taught, 'The special office of the Holy Ghost is to enlighten and ennoble the mind, to purify and sanctify the soul, to incite to good works, and to reveal the things of God.'"[5]

Parley P. Pratt explains: "The gift of the Holy Ghost...quickens all the intellectual faculties, increases, enlarges, expands, and purifies all the natural passions and affections; and adapts them, by the gift of wisdom, to their lawful use. It inspires, develops, cultivates and matures all the fine-tones of sympathies, joys, tastes, kindred feelings, and affections of our nature. It inspires virtue, kindness, goodness, tenderness, gentleness, and charity. It develops beauty of person, form and features. It tends to health, vigor, animation, and social feeling. It invigorates all the faculties of the physical and intellectual man. It strengthens, and gives tone to the nerves. In short, it is, as it were, marrow to the bone, joy to the heart, light to the eyes, music to the ears, and life to the whole being."[6]

If we take the time to cultivate and nurture the Spirit's companionship, the power of the Holy Ghost will be a tremendous influence in our lives.

Learning to Hear and Follow the Holy Ghost

So, how do we know when the Spirit is communicating with us? A friend provided what I think is a wonderful analogy: When it is of the Spirit, meaning when something is right and good, it feels like "a sponge soaking up water." When it is not of the Spirit, it is like "waves crashing against rocks."

In section nine of the Doctrine and Covenants, revelation given to Joseph Smith tells us how one can know if something is right. "And if it is right I will cause that your bosom shall burn within you; therefore, you shall feel that it is right. But if it be not right you shall have no such feelings, but you shall have a stupor of thought that shall cause you to forget the thing which is wrong" (D&C 9:8–9).

When something is right there is a sense of calmness and peace within, like it fits. Joseph Smith says, we "feel that it is right," and as my friend says, like "a sponge soaking up water." However, if something is not right, we have "a stupor of thought" or a feeling like "waves crashing against rocks." We feel confused, not sure about the situation. We feel negative, or the idea fades away. In these cases, we know to back away from the decision we were making.

But what about those times when it is not so obvious, when the answer is not right there in front of us, and we do not have a clear feeling one way or the other?

The same section in the Doctrine and Covenants outlines this perfectly as well. First, we must do the homework by studying the issue out in our own mind. Heavenly Father leaves it for us to gather the information, and study and ponder to a point of making a decision. Then we take that decision to God in prayer for a confirmation. If it is right, we will have the feelings described above. If it is not right, we will remain confused.

Many of us wait for Heavenly Father to tell us what to do and then wonder why we have no answers to our prayers. However, if we have not come up with a plan or conclusion, what can God confirm? If we go to Him with no plan, He cannot give us a good feeling about something, because we have not presented Him with anything. But if we study the situation until we have a solution to the problem, when we take that to Him, if it is right, we will feel a sense of peace. But if it is wrong, we will feel a barrier, be confused, or the idea will fade away.

During a doctor's visit Bob was told he needed a five-bypass heart surgery—something not to take lightly. Just a few years ago many died from such open-heart surgeries. Bob knew he did not have to have the surgery, but that he was at high risk for a heart attack if he chose not to have the bypass.

Bob pondered what to do, knowing risk went with either decision. One evening after praying about his dilemma, Bob decided to go ahead with the surgery. He woke up in the early morning hours and felt a strong but peaceful assurance regarding his decision and that everything would work out for the best. Bob went through with the surgery with no concern, because the Spirit bore a strong and powerful witness to him that all would be well. All did go well.

If we do not have a clear confirmation but have studied the problem and made a good decision based on our study, and do not have a "stupor of thought" or feel like "the water is crashing against rocks," we need to follow that path. Sometimes it is not until after the trial of our faith that we receive the witness and blessing.[7]

If the path we choose turns out wrong, yet we are living in a manner that allows the Spirit's influence in our lives, we will discover roadblocks or that the situation simply does not work out. Knowing our Father in Heaven has our best interests in mind and knows all, we can trust He is leading our way. We then need to restudy the situation, choose again, and seek His confirmation.

We also know by the fruits of the situation if it is of God and of the Spirit. If the situation leads to goodness, growth, faith, Godliness, or a better way of doing things, it is of God and of the Spirit. If the event or action tears us or others down, leads to darkness, confusion or worry, it is not of the Spirit.

Life is complicated enough without adding avoidable mistakes. The Spirit will lead us around those mistakes to a more fulfilling and peaceful life if we will seek the Spirit's counsel and trust its power and influence. In our day and age, it is not only worthwhile but vital.

How to Tell If We Have the Holy Ghost

How do we know if we have the Spirit? The table on the next page shows specific characteristics.

We know we have the Spirit in our lives by the fruits of its influence. If we feel angry, have a negative attitude, withdraw from others, or any other characteristic identified with not having the Spirit, we need to see if our thoughts and actions would make a heavenly messenger such as the Spirit feel welcome. If not, our best interest would be to rid ourselves of that which stands in the way of the Spirit's influence.

The power of the Holy Ghost is real. As we nurture our relationship with the Spirit, we will develop the positive attributes described above. We will notice its influence and have an acute awareness when its presence is lacking in our lives. We will be guided through trials and "know the truth of all things," including the reasons why we are where we are in life and the steps we need to take moment-by-moment, day-by-day, year-by-year. With the Holy Spirit in our lives, we are blessed, taken care of, and are *not alone*.

When the Spirit Is in Our Lives	When the Spirit Is Not in Our Lives
Sense of fulfillment	Sense of emptiness (something is missing)
Calm	Easily frustrated
Peace	Easily irritated, angry
Confidence	Discouraged easily
Full of light, joy	Heavy and dark
Genuinely happy	Depressed
Aware of others and their needs	Self-centered
Generous, patient, tolerant, want to give selfless service	Self-absorbed and selfish
Enjoy the success of others	Competitive, jealous, envious of others
No one offends you	Easily offended
Speak well of others	Critical of others
Desire to help others	Desire to get even
Peaceful even when things around you are not	Need to be filled by earthly things
Desire to keep commandments	Commandments are too strict or unnecessary
Trust the word of God more than men	Trust the word of men more than God
Enjoy the company of others	Tendency to withdraw from others
Desire to be with those you love	Desire to be alone
Willing to offer Church service	Lack of desire to serve in Church callings
Generally do acts of kindness unbeknownst to others	Desire for others to notice your acts of service
Generally trust the goodness of others	Question others' motives
Desire to follow the promptings of the Spirit	Confused
Sure of the truthfulness of the existence of God	Question the truthfulness of the existence of God
Positive attitude	Negative attitude

Notes

1. James E. Faust, "The Gift of the Holy Ghost—A Sure Compass," *Ensign*, May 1989, 32–33.

2. *History of the Church*, 3:379.

3. Brigham Young, *Deseret News Weekly*, 9 February, 1854, 4.

4. Carlos E. Asay, "The Companionship of the Holy Ghost," *Ensign*, April 1988, 17.

5. L.Tom Perry, *Living with Enthusiasm*, 44.

6. Parley P. Pratt, *Key to the Science of Theology*, 9th ed. (1965), 101.

7. Spencer W. Kimball, *Faith Precedes the Miracle*.

Part Two
THE PATH

Chapter Seven

EXPECT DARKNESS, MERCY, AND LIGHT

"I PERCEIVE THAT YE ARE IN THE PATH of righteousness; I perceive that ye are in the path which leads to the kingdom of God; yea I perceive that ye are making his path straight" (Alma 7:19). When we choose to follow Christ, we enter into "the path."

The path, although narrow and straight (see Matthew 7:14), has definite "road markers" which can confuse us if we are not expecting them or are not aware of them. If we are on the path, we can be assured there is a purpose for what we experience along the way. However, understanding these road markers helps ease the journey.

Lehi, a prophet in the Book of Mormon, offers insight into these signposts and what often happens when we choose to follow Christ. Let us look at what happened to Lehi after the Savior appeared to him in his dream (see 1 Nephi 8:5–6):

"And it came to pass that I saw a man, and he was dressed in a white robe; and he came and stood before me. And it came to pass that he spake unto me, and bade me follow him."

Imagine the Savior standing before you bidding you to follow Him. First of all, would you recognize Him if He did not have some specific way to show His true identity? Secondly, would you follow? Lehi does.

Verse 7 continues: "And it came to pass that as I followed him I beheld myself that I was in a dark and dreary waste."

Wait one minute! It's not supposed to be dark and dreary. Isn't it supposed to be wonderful when we choose to follow Christ? Lehi meets the Savior, heeds His call to follow, then suddenly finds himself in darkness! Is that the way the story is supposed to go? Let us read on.

Verse 8: "And after I had traveled for the space of many hours in darkness, I began to pray unto the Lord that he would have mercy on me, according to the multitude of his tender mercies."

And verse 9: "And it came to pass after I had prayed unto the Lord I beheld a large and spacious field."

Initially, this may not seem significant, but what a powerful moment. As we understand by the implication of darkness, Lehi could not see his way. Not until Lehi "prays" for "mercy" and Heavenly Father intervenes, is he able to see what is around him. After hours in darkness, he is finally able to see. Imagine Lehi's relief!

Lehi describes three road markers we all encounter in life, at one time or another, when we choose to follow Christ:

1. **We will experience darkness.** It may come sooner rather than later. It may happen many times. Each time may prove a greater challenge than the previous one. Nevertheless, it comes. Darkness is part of the plan.

2. **We will need to call upon the Lord's "tender mercies."** At some point in our lives, and in order to make it through our trials, we will need to call upon the Lord's help.

3. **We will receive the light necessary to see the way.** When we call upon the Lord we will receive the light to see our way. The light may be just enough to see our next step but it will be there to show us the way.

Let us look more closely at the significance of each marker.

ROAD MARKER ONE—EXPECT DARKNESS

Remember the Young Men and Women program (MIA or Mutual for a lot of us). In some odd way, many of us learned, or thought we heard, that if we lived according to the gospel plan and did what we were supposed to do, we would live "happily ever after." I do not remember being told about the frustrations, conflicts, or pains in life. In fact, I thought I learned that if we lived our lives righteously, we would avoid pain and be happy. Well, however the message was taught or however we heard it, many of us got it wrong. Pain, conflict, frustration, and disappointments are *all* a part of the plan. In fact, adversity is an essential part of the plan.

I wonder if Lehi was surprised when he found himself in darkness, especially right after the Savior's beckoning call to follow. I wonder if his initial thoughts might have been something like, "Hey, the Savior asked me to follow Him. I bet we'll see angels, float on clouds, and have a good time." I wonder if, even for a moment, Lehi felt betrayed or overwhelmed.

I wonder, too, what must have been going through Lehi's mind during his time in the "dark and dreary waste." Did he feel scared, alone, or abandoned? Was he confused, not knowing which way to turn? How could he find his way in darkness? As "dreary waste" implies, he must have felt the emptiness, the nothingness.

Obviously, Lehi had faith, trusting that God knew what He was doing even when Lehi felt left alone to walk in the dark. It must have taken great strength, courage, humility, and wisdom to turn to the Lord for help.

Why Darkness?

So, why is there darkness if we're living right, keeping the commandments, and doing what we are supposed to do? Isn't God supposed to bless us? Isn't He supposed to give us what we want—a job, a car, a date, a life?! Instead, we get this "dreary waste," or so it seems. And in our finite minds it just does not make sense. Let us look at some possible reasons for adversity.

To Give Us Experience

Perhaps darkness helps us gain experience so we can be more like Christ (see D&C 22:7). The classic example is Joseph Smith's account while in Liberty jail. God said to him, "And if thou shouldst be cast into the pit, or into the hands of murderers, and the sentence of death passed upon thee; if thou be cast into the deep; if the billowing surge conspire against thee; if fierce winds become thine enemy; if the heavens gather blackness, and all the elements combine to hedge up the way; and above all, if the very jaws of hell shall gape open the mouth wide after thee, know thou, my son, *that all these things shall give thee experience*, and shall be for thy good. The Son of Man hath descended below them all. Art thou greater than he?…therefore, fear not what man can do, for God shall be with you forever and ever." (D&C 122:7–9, emphasis added). Imagine any one of those events happening to us in our lives.

These challenges can contribute to our growth. Such growth brings maturity, seasoning, and understanding of truth and wisdom. It is not the numbers of trials we meet, but the trials we overcome in Christlike ways that make us triumphant. What greater quest and opportunities are there than to use our earthly experiences for this purpose?

To Teach a Lesson

Should darkness continue, we can examine what eternal principle the experience offers.

Damian experienced what to him was a long, dark period in his life. Following his father's death, many pressures unfairly vied for Damian's energy and emotional support. His mother and siblings relied on him to help ease their grief. His boss continuously expected him to work harder and longer for little pay. Damian also felt pressure from his priesthood responsibility to date and to marry. He became emotionally drained when a relationship ended he had hoped would result in marriage. Trying to juggle these demands, Damian had little leisure time and, consequently, few friends.

Concerned with his physical and mental health, Damian prayed to God to somehow lighten his load. However, it did not happen. Damian's stress only increased with more pressure from work and his family. The growing loneliness and fatigue caused Damian to stay home and sleep most weekends. Drained, unsupported, and overwhelmed, he felt as if he were on his last limping leg.

Contemplating his situation, Damian realized God could relieve him of his burden, but he also realized that he would set himself up again to be pulled off balance, as was his plight in the past. He began to take serious stock of his situation and of his own hand in controlling his circumstances. Damian decided to call upon God for help while forcing himself to set healthy boundaries, create balance in his life, and take better care of himself.

Allowing Damian to find the answers for himself helped him make his own life richer and more fulfilling. What might have been a temporary change became life changing.

Oddly, it is through adversity that we grow. The bigger the dilemma, the bigger potential for growth. Through our trials, we learn the very lessons needed to complete our missions here on earth.

I am convinced if we do not learn a lesson the first time around, we will re-experience the same situation again and again until we learn the lesson and break the cycle. So when caught in a harmful or frustrating pattern of living, consider looking for the lesson to be learned and strive to make the necessary changes. Looking inside ourselves and asking, "What can I change within me to stop the cycle?" can be difficult, even painful, but remember that with God all things are possible (see Matthew 19:26). This is the way we move beyond our limitations and grow.

To Build Faith

Perhaps the challenge we face is meant to strengthen our faith. "Whosoever putteth his trust in him the same shall be lifted up at the last day" (Mosiah 23:22).

A wonderful example of faith is demonstrated in the story of the widow who gave what was left of her last meal to the prophet Elijah when he asked for food. Expecting she and her son would die, she said,

"As the Lord thy God liveth, I have not a cake, but an handful of meal in a barrel, and a little oil in a cruse: and, behold, I am gathering two sticks, that I may go in and dress it for me and my son, that we may eat it, and die. And Elijah said unto her, Fear not; go and do as thou hast said: but make me thereof a little cake first, and bring it unto me, and after make for thee and for they son. For thus saith the Lord God of Israel, The barrel of meal shall not waste, neither shall the cruse of oil fail, until the day that the Lord sendeth rain upon the earth" (1 Kings 17:12–14). Choosing to believe the words of Elijah, in obedience she fed him.

The scriptures tell us the story's end. "And the barrel of meal wasted not, neither did the cruse of oil fail, according to the word of the Lord, which he spake by Elijah" (1 Kings 17:16). Because of her faith, she and her son did not die but were blessed with all the food and oil they needed.

God asks us to live by faith and trust Him. Proverbs 3:5 reads, "Trust in the Lord with all thine heart, and lean not unto thine own understanding." This is extremely tough to do in a day and age when it is hard to trust anyone around us. But remember this is not just anyone. It is God. He even said we should not trust in the "arm of flesh." Why? Because trusting in the arm of flesh will disappoint us. You see, we are all imperfect and if given enough time in each other's presence, we will reveal our imperfections and cause disappointment. As a result we may curse God; however, God had nothing to do with it. We simply misplaced our trust— in the arm of flesh and not in God. Only He is "perfect."

President Howard W. Hunter said at a devotional speech, "Please remember this one thing. If our lives and our faith are centered upon Jesus Christ and His restored gospel, nothing can ever go permanently wrong. On the other hand, if our lives are not centered on the Savior and his teachings, no other success can ever be permanently right."[1]

You see, when we speak of faith in Christ, we mean we trust His teachings of hope, charity, peace, and believe His word when He says He cares (see 1 Peter 5:7). It is the pure love of Christ that delivers us peace, knowing He cares and is concerned—and that He can cure and ease any burden we carry with His healing power. In addition, if He does not cure or ease our burden, we know there is a purpose for it, because we know He loves us and wants what is best for us.

We too are often asked to walk to the "edge" of our faith, as Elijah asked of the widow. "Wherefore, dispute not because ye see not, for ye receive no witness until after the trial of your faith"

(Ether 12:6). We may be asked to take one step at a time, not knowing what might come later. These are the moments we may not understand and nothing in our lives makes sense. Nevertheless, if we live righteously and follow the Spirit, we can trust that there is a purpose for our experience, and that all will be for our good.

Opposition in All Things

We are told, "For it must needs be that there is an opposition in all things. If not so,... righteousness could not be brought to pass, neither wickedness, neither holiness, nor misery, neither good nor bad" (2 Nephi 2:11). In other words, there must be bad in order for there to be good. President Spencer W. Kimball said, "Should all prayers be immediately answered according to our selfish desires and our limited understanding, then there would be little or no suffering, sorrow, disappointment, or even death, and if these were not, there would also be no joy, success, resurrection, nor eternal life and godhood." He goes on to say, "There would be no test of strength, no development of character, no growth of powers, no free agency."[2]

What a glorious plan. How else would we understand the heights of joy, happiness, peace, and the best of life if we never understood or experienced some of the worst of life? During those painful moments, we may not think it is so wonderful. However, when we endure and grow beyond the trials, we appreciate the growth and learning, as well as the development of strength and character. And, although we usually do not wish to repeat the ordeal, how we value the resultant goodness when it enters our lives!

A Proving Ground

Perhaps darkness is a proving ground to help determine real intent. How serious are we about seeking God in our lives or are we looking for a quick escape? In Abraham 3:23 we read, "We will prove them herewith to see if they will do all things whatsoever the Lord their God shall command them" (D&C 98:12–14).

Nobody knows better than Abraham about God's testing. God asked Abraham to sacrifice his son. It must have been agonizing, but Abraham was willing to do what God asked. Only in the very act of sacrificing his son did God stop Abraham and say, "Lay not thine hand upon the lad, neither do thou any thing unto him: for now I know that thou fearest God, seeing thou hast not withheld thy son, thine only son from me" (Genesis 22:12).

Maybe God is intent upon seeing how serious we are in following Him, because He promises all He has to us. "My people must be tried in all things, that they may be prepared to receive the glory that I have for them" (D&C 136:31). Maybe these trials are to help us know if we are ready to handle that glory. And if we are not, the very experience will help prepare us.

Talking to singles about the absence of family in their lives, President Kimball stated, "On occasions when you ache for that acceptance and affection which belong to family life on earth, please know that our Father in Heaven is aware of your anguish," (darkness as it were), "and that one day He will bless you beyond your capacity to express. Sometimes to be tested and proved requires that we be temporarily deprived but righteous women and men will one day receive all—think of it—all that our Father has. It is not only worth waiting for; it is worth living for."[3]

How Darkness Shows Up

Darkness can show up in many ways. Much of the time it is our own actions that end up creating a separation between God and ourselves. Sin, pride, self-centeredness, and the misuse of agency all create barriers to God. Such obstructions to light perpetuate darkness.

The actions of others can plunge us into darkness. God gave us agency, and part of that freedom means we are allowed to make good or bad choices. When someone chooses wrongly and it effects us in a negative way, the Savior is aware and weeps—just as He did at the grave of Lazarus, or over Jerusalem's afflictions, or when He knelt with the people in America (see 3 Nephi 17:21–22; John 11:35; Luke 19:41). He feels the pain. But He will not intervene or override agency because these choices determine our ultimate destiny.

For example, if God constantly stops a person who has a murderous heart from murdering, just to avoid anyone getting hurt, this person's true intentions would never be exposed. Heavenly Father has to allow such events to happen because, in the end, it will be those very actions that condemn the offender. On Judgment Day, when the "great movie" is played and all is made known, our true character will be revealed.

In some cases darkness translates into being without clue, unaware, or lacking understanding. Have you ever shared a gospel principle with someone who was unable to understand what you were talking about? You knew the truth of the principle and saw clearly their lack of understanding. Your truth did not change, even when they did not understand. They simply were not on a spiritual level to comprehend what you were trying to share.

We are often in this same kind of darkness—not yet on a level to fully understand any number of circumstances. We might complain or make up reasons, using earthly commentaries, scientific evidence, or our own limited understanding. Our own thinking may prove very creative, but may not represent truth.

Driven by our limited understanding, we ask, "Why, God, art thou letting this happen?" However, we must remember to "lean not unto (our) own understanding" (Proverbs 3:5), for God's thoughts are not our thoughts (see Isaiah 55:8).

Darkness can come into our lives through simply living. This is a natural part of mortality. Sometimes the unexpected and accidents just happen. They happen because we live in an imperfect world with car accidents, injuries, and death. There is not always an obvious purpose, but, though His hand be stayed, our Father in Heaven is there. It may be our "moment of truth" in which to grow and show what we are made of. If we are not yet made of what we need to be, then what we are experiencing—if we allow it through Heavenly Father's influence in our life—will help create that which we lack (see Ether 12:27).

Rarely does God smite us with affliction, but there are times in the Bible when this has, in fact, happened. Speaking of the world today, Nephi predicted, "For the kingdom of the devil must shake, and they which belong to it must needs be stirred up unto repentance, or the devil will grasp them with his everlasting chains" (2 Nephi 28:19).

Sometimes a little darkness helps to remind us about what really matters, "except the Lord doth chasten his people with many afflictions, they will not remember him" (Helaman 12:3).

To Learn to Depend on God

Perhaps the most important reason we have darkness is to bring us to God. How else or why else would we feel the need for Him? If life were fine and there were no trials, we would be under an illusion of not needing God.

There are moments when we are taken beyond our limits and understanding and feel we no longer can continue on our own. It is then that we need something or someone else to provide what we cannot do for ourselves. Through the grace of our Savior we can receive the light needed to move forward beyond the darkness. Of course, we can choose to stay where we are, rely on ourselves, and potentially live in misery and pain. God will not force anyone into divine dependency. However, if we want to grow we must learn to depend on God. Through our willingness to ask for His help and then follow His lead, we will grow spiritually and then successfully make it through the difficult times in our lives.

How Long Must We Endure?

No one can say how long moments of darkness will last. Even after we have passed through one difficult period, there may be more to come. Some challenges in life are not going to be resolved here on earth. Paul carried "a thorn in the flesh." He asked three times for it to be removed. The Savior said to him, "My grace is sufficient for thee: for my strength is made perfect in weakness" (2 Corinthians 12:7–9). The Savior gave Paul what he needed to compensate for his limitations so Paul could live a meaningful life. Perhaps the very thorn in his side made Paul the man he needed to be to end up an Apostle of Jesus Christ.

Some of us may not receive the rewards we seek in this life, although we are promised that if we remain faithful, they will come in the next. Life often requires us to focus on the eternal perspective and to look beyond the narrow vision of our mortal life alone. It helps to remember we are spiritual beings experiencing, for a time, a mortal existence.

Becca, now in her thirties, learned at twelve that she had multiple sclerosis. She is now completely dependent on others. Her physical burden, more than likely, will not be lifted in this lifetime. Nevertheless, Becca has the faith to continue even in the midst of adversity. She gave a talk at a fireside, having been rolled into the chapel on a bed. Unable to move without pain, barely able to turn the pages of her notes, she illuminated those who were in other kinds of darkness. Her example was the most powerful message, to not only endure, but to endure well through our life's struggles. Those who attended that meeting were never to be the same.

C. S. Lewis said, "The cross comes before the crown. It is not our time table to decide when the cross has been completely born. It is our responsibility to bear it."[4]

Darkness As a Blessing

Paul spoke boldly to the Romans about dark moments when he said, "But glory in tribulations... knowing that tribulation worketh patience; and patience, experience; and experience, hope" (Romans 5:3–5). Paul taught the Corinthians, "For our light affliction, which is but for a moment, worketh for us a far more exceeding and eternal weight of glory" (2 Corinthians 4:17).

With an eternal perspective, we realize that as long as we live close to our Father in Heaven's will, there is no negative experience in this life, for each one helps us become more like God Himself. Lehi, talking to his son Jacob, said, "Thou knowest the greatness of God; and He shall consecrate thine afflictions for thy gain" (2 Nephi 2:2).

The question becomes, "What are we willing to endure to enjoy the ultimate peace and joy in this life as well as in the world to come?" Determination and patience are required as we go through darkness. If we remain steadfast through critical moments of darkness, we will experience freedom, wisdom, peace, and understanding.

Tribulation Comes to All

As the story goes, a woman approached President Harold B. Lee after a talk at BYU expressing how she wished she were an apostle. When he asked why, she responded, "Because up there you are closer to God and must have a pretty easy-going life." At the time, President Lee's daughter had just passed away, leaving six children. Three years earlier, his wife had died, and as president of the Church, he had the weight of the Church on his shoulders. It was anything but an easy-going life for President Lee.[5]

A truth in life is that the rain falls on the just and the unjust. Every one of us will experience times that are exacting, unfair, and shake us to our core. And it has nothing to do with whether we are good or bad, or if we are in high places of authority in the Church as in President Lee's situation.

The reality is that the closer we are to God, sometimes the greater the trials will be—as in Job's case, who was very close to God and yet suffered the most extreme moments of darkness. It is part of the purifying and sanctifying process (see 3 Nephi 24:2–3).

As we grow close to God we develop a greater appreciation for the dark periods in our lives. We grow in humility and in understanding which helps us better endure adversity. When we understand the "whys" and have the openness to trust, it is much easier to handle the "whats" and "hows" of any situation.

Joseph Smith, while in the Liberty Jail, asked God, "O God, where art thou? And where is the pavilion that covereth thy hiding place? How long shall thy hand be stayed?" Joseph was told, "My son, peace be unto thy soul; thine adversity and thine afflictions shall be but a small moment; and if thou endure it well, God shall exalt thee on high; thou shalt triumph over all thy foes." God, putting it in perspective for Joseph, said, "Thou are not yet as Job" (D&C 121: 1–2, 7–8, 10). Joseph was left in the dark for a time for his growth and experience.

However, the greatest example is that of the Savior in the Garden of Gethsemane, asking to have the bitter cup removed, but only if it were the will of God the Father. He, then, being humiliated and tortured, suffered, bled, and died upon the cross for every man, woman, and child. He suffered greater pain than any of us can imagine. Every heartache and pain we experience, He experienced, only with far greater intensity. In fact, He who was the greatest among us was, for the moment, the least. It was not because God the Father did not love His Son. It was because He loved us, every one of us, that He allowed His Only Begotten Son to suffer such pain and go through this exquisitely profound moment of darkness.

In our efforts to become like Christ, should we feel ourselves exempt from the same? "The Son of Man hath descended below them all. Art thou greater than He?" (D&C 122:8). From His darkness comes our light.

ROAD MARKER TWO—SEEKING HEAVENLY FATHER AND MERCY THROUGH THE ATONEMENT OF CHRIST

Now let's turn to Lehi's dream: Lehi follows the Savior, immediately finds himself in darkness, and then something amazing happens! Maybe Lehi thought he shouldn't ask or maybe it took a while before dawning on Lehi to ask, or perhaps he was trying to understand it on his own, but for whatever reason, it took "many hours" before Lehi prayed asking for the Father's "tender mercies." What a wonderful way to say, "Help!" Not only did Lehi show understanding of the true nature of the Father when he recognized His mercy as "tender," but also Lehi shows a very humble side of himself when he said to the Father, "I need help." This is road marker two on our path—our turning to God and seeking His mercy.

Maybe the Father wanted Lehi to practice faith and was waiting for Lehi to have a pure heart and real intent (see James 10:3–5). Nevertheless, it was only when Lehi prayed that the Savior came and provided Lehi with the light to see his way.

Unfortunately, like Lehi, we can spend hours, even days, weeks, or years in the dark, feeling frustrated, and blaming God. Look at the Israelites who wandered for forty years before they got it right with the Lord. Only when we realize our own limitations and call upon our Father in Heaven will He bestow His mercy upon us. "Thus doth the Lord work with his power in all cases among the children of men, extending the arm of mercy towards them that put their trust in Him" (Mosiah 29:20). "Behold, he sendeth an invitation unto all men, for the arms of mercy are extended towards them" (Alma 5:33).

Seeking Mercy

We seek mercy for many different reasons. We seek mercy for forgiveness to become free from the bondage of sin and wrong doing. So much pain can come from making poor choices. Others seek mercy for greater understanding, particularly when confused or overwhelmed. Sometimes we plead for the removal of a sore trial, or at least for a brief respite. When this does not happen, we cry for greater strength and patience to endure the difficult task or burden, as Alma prayed, "O Lord, my heart is exceedingly sorrowful; wilt thou comfort my soul in Christ. O Lord, wilt thou grant unto me that I may have strength, that I may suffer with patience these afflictions which shall come upon me?" (Alma 31:31). Sometimes we cry for faith, support, comfort, and peace, especially during those moments when we are afraid, without hope, or lonely.

We say, "God, I need thee. I need thy mercy, help, and understanding." As we hand over the situation to Him, our life's challenges and circumstances may not change. The next day may not look any different from the day before. Nevertheless, if we are sincere in our efforts, a change within begins and our burden begins to lift. We are given the mercy and vision we seek and the needed faith to follow.

Alma the younger personally understood the power of God's

mercy. For three days and nights, Alma felt "racked, even with the pains of a damned soul." But, remembering his father's prophesy concerning the coming of Jesus Christ, he said, "I cried within my heart: O Jesus, thou Son of God, have mercy on me, who am in the gall of bitterness, and am encircled about by the everlasting chains of death." Alma's sincere prayer continues, "And...when I thought this, I could remember my pains no more, yea, I was harrowed up by the memory of my sins no more" (Alma 36:18–19). Alma received God's mercy and his life was changed.

Darkness, in any form, is bondage. We are blinded, unable to see where to go. God will deliver us out of that bondage if we turn to Him and ask for His help. Perhaps the hard part is humbling ourselves enough to ask.

We can spend our lives studying the philosophies of the world trying to reach the "light" through an endless study of the "dark." However, in the end, there is only one path (see Romans 5:15), and that is calling upon God and His "tender" mercies. Only with His mercy will we move beyond the darkness.

ROAD MARKER THREE—THE LIGHT

Just as our Father in Heaven gave Lehi light so he could see his way, so will He do for each one of us if we ask Him. "Then spake Jesus again unto them, saying, I am the light of the world: he that followeth me shall not walk in darkness, but shall have the light of life" (John 8:12). This is road marker three—receiving light to see the way.

Notice the Savior did not take Lehi out of the situation nor walk the path for him. Instead, He gave Lehi light so he had better perspective and could choose with more clarity. Fortunately, Lehi followed the path shown him. What relief he must have felt finally having light when everything had been so dark.

Describing King Lamoni's experience with light, Alma records, "The dark veil of unbelief was being cast away from his mind, and the light which did light up his mind, which was the light of the Glory of God…yea, this light had infused such joy unto his soul, the cloud of darkness having been dispelled, and the light of everlasting life was lit up in his soul" (Alma 19:16).

We can dispel darkness from our lives. Paul encouraged the Romans to do so: "The night is far spent, the day is at hand: let us therefore cast off the works of darkness, and let us put on the armor of light" (Romans 13:12). When we allow the light of Christ to illuminate our souls, we experience relief and joy. "For the word of the Lord is truth, and whatsoever is truth is light, and whatsoever is light is Spirit, even the Spirit of Jesus Christ" (D&C 84:45). Our life fills with light, truth, and His spirit.

How Light Shows Up

The Savior's light illuminates in many ways. Perhaps the most profound is the light we receive when we implement the Atonement of Jesus Christ. The Savior took upon Himself every sin ever committed so we may be cleansed and made whole. For those who are sincere in their cries for mercy and truly repent and seek forgiveness, assurance will come that God forgives and forgets.

In some cases we may need to make restitution and, with more serious sins, we may need to confess to priesthood authority. Nevertheless, "Behold, he who has repented of his sins, the same is forgiven, and I, the Lord, remember them no more" (D&C 58:42). Once we have access to the light of Christ and its influence, we are free from the sins of the past. We can see the path before us, and new life begins.

Alma, receiving mercy and forgiveness for his past sins, describes his experience, "I was in the darkest abyss, but now I behold the marvelous light of God" (Mosiah 27:29). Teaching his son about the joy of being "born of God" (Alma 36:5), Alma continues, "And oh, what joy, and what marvelous light I did behold; yea my soul was filled with joy as exceeding as was my pain! Yea,…there could be nothing so exquisite and so bitter as were my pains. Yea,…on the other hand, there can be nothing so exquisite and sweet as was my joy" (Alma 36:20–21). Peace awaits us as the burden of sin lifts, and the Light of the Savior's influence fills our souls.

Light as Understanding

As mentioned earlier, darkness translates into being clueless. Hence, light is what gives us understanding. Proverbs 3:13 reads, "Happy is the man that findeth wisdom and the man that getteth understanding." For "…if ye will enter in by the way, and receive the Holy Ghost, it will show you all things what ye should do" (2 Nephi 32:3,5).

Just as God cast His light onto darkness both physically and spiritually in the parable of the blind man (see John 9), so He does with us. "I say it that you may know the truth, that you may chase darkness from among you" (D&C 50:25). His Spirit illuminates our spiritual eyes (see Moses 6:27), enlightens our minds, and quickens our understanding. We see the way before us, the eternal perspective, and what we could not see before. The mere understanding often increases our ability to cope.

Light as Faith

Light also comes in the form of faith. Jesus told His disciples, "ye now therefore have sorrow: but I will see you again, and your heart shall rejoice, and your joy no man taketh from you" (John 16:22). Things happen that we do not understand. Instead of complaining and rejecting God, we can trust that He knows what He is doing and that there is a purpose for our experience. If we ask in prayer what we need to learn in order to grow beyond this particular challenge, listen intently, and then follow the inspiration given, we gain understanding and our faith grows.

The key is to remain faithful, trusting there is a reason and purpose. Until we reach a higher level of understanding, we can apply faith, knowing that for "everything there is a season, and a time to every purpose under the heaven" (Ecclesiastes 3:1).

Light as Comfort

Light provides comfort and peace, and the ability to cope. "Whosoever shall put their trust in God shall be supported in their trials and their troubles and their afflictions and shall be lifted up at the last day" (Alma 36:3). Alma explained to his son Shiblon: "But behold, I did cry unto him and I did find peace to my soul" (Alma 38:8).

The Savior said, "I will never leave thee nor forsake thee" (Hebrews 13:5). He blessed us when He said, "Peace I leave with you, my peace I give unto you; not as the world giveth, give I unto you....These things I have spoken unto you, that in me ye might have peace" (John 14:27; 16:33).

Our Father in Heaven will lighten our load and provide comfort when we align our life with the light of Christ. "I will ease your burdens which are put upon your shoulders, that even you can not feel them upon your backs, even while you are in bondage" (Mosiah 24:14). As we give our burdens to God, our part becomes "light and easy" because our focus is now on following His commandments, listening, and following the promptings of the Holy Spirit.

Light as a Guide

"I will be your light…and I will prepare the way before you, if it so be that ye shall keep my commandments" (1 Nephi 17:13).

His light is like a "lamp unto [our] feet" (Psalms 119: 105), "to guide our feet into the way of peace" (Luke 1:78–79).

President Thomas S. Monson once said, "As you walk through life, always walk toward the light, and the shadows of life will fall behind you."[6]

Our journey is taken one step at a time. If we seek our Father in Heaven in prayer, He will give us the light to show us the way, even if it only illuminates our next step. What a wonderful gift to have a light within that shows us the way, even when we may not know the destination.

To Wake Unto God

Perhaps the greatest gift of the light is to bring us into the glow of God and His love. "Behold, he changed their hearts yea he awakened them out of a deep sleep, and they awoke unto God. Behold they were in the midst of darkness; nevertheless, their souls were illuminated by the light of the everlasting word.... Yea they were loosed, and their souls did expand, and they did sing redeeming love" (Alma 5:7–9).

God's light awakens us from the deep sleep which sin, fear and pride create. "He is the light and the life of the world: yea, a light that is endless, that can never be darkened" (Mosiah 16:9). When we seek God's mercy, we will receive His light. Awake, we understand His goodness and the greatness of life. It is through His light that we experience His redeeming love.

ROAD MARKER FOUR—GOING FORTH AND PARTAKING

We could end our discussion about Lehi's dream right here having learned a great truth about life and the processes of God— that darkness is a part of our earthly experience, and that when we look to Christ, we will be given light to see the way. However, not looking further into Lehi's dream would deny us the best part of the journey—the icing on the cake.

You see, receiving God's light is only the beginning. There is so much more if we are willing to put forth the effort, as illustrated in the rest of Lehi's story:

We read in verse 10, "And it came to pass that I beheld a tree, whose fruit was desirable to make one happy. And it came to pass that I did go forth and partake of the fruit there of."

When Lehi prayed, he received light that illuminated the path ahead of him. This vision gave Lehi perspective so he could make choices good for him. Notice that Lehi did not stop with just having the light and the vision of the path, but he went forth and partook of what was there before him—the fruit.

Now, the icing on the cake: Verse 11 reads, "...and I beheld that it was the most sweet, above all that I ever before tasted. Yea and I beheld that the fruit thereof was white, to exceed all the whiteness that I had ever seen."

There are some very "sweet" and pure moments in life—the birth of a baby, family occasions, time with friends and loved ones, and more. But Lehi says that this experience was sweeter, purer, "above all that [he] ever before tasted...to exceed all...that [he] had ever seen." Lehi not only says it is sweeter and purer than anything he ever experienced, but look what else happens.

Continuing with verse 12, "And as I partook of the fruit thereof it filled my soul with exceeding great joy."

This whole experience fills. Not full, like after a big meal, but Lehi's soul filled "with exceeding great joy." Have you experienced this? Do you know what he is talking about?

Once the light illuminates the path, we must make the effort to follow—do the walking, stretching, reaching, and partaking of what is set before us. This is the fourth road marker on our path to follow Christ—going forth and partaking—not always easy, and in fact, can be quite challenging. It requires commitment, dedication, long suffering, and steadfastness.

You may say, "To what do we go forth? Of what do we partake? I don't see a tree."

Notes

1. Howard W. Hunter, "Fear Not, Little Flock," in *Brigham Young University 1988–89 Devotional and Fireside Speeches,* (1989), 112.

2. Spencer W. Kimball, *Faith Precedes the Miracle,* 97.

3. Spencer W. Kimball, "The Role of Righteous Women," *Ensign,* November 1979, 103.

4. C. S. Lewis, *The Weight of Glory*—copyright © C.S. Lewis Pte. Ltd. 1949. Extracts reprinted by permission.

5. Brent Top, BYU Education Week, 1987.

6. Thomas S. Monson, *Your Journey to Eternal Joy* (pamphlet, address given at a Young Women fireside, 18 October 1987), 12.

Chapter Eight

GOING FORTH AND PARTAKING

WHEN WE CHOOSE TO FOLLOW the Savior, having humility and real intent, He will illuminate the steps and personalize details in the process to better know Him and become like He is. By following those steps, we overcome personal shortcomings and develop characteristics like those of the Savior—to love as He loves, care as He cares, and follow our Father in Heaven as He follows Him.

Settle This in Your Heart

The process is not easy and some refuse to "go forth" on the path and "partake." They may know the truth, are baptized, have the Light and Holy Spirit in their lives, and can even see the steps ahead to take, but still choose to not go forth. It is as if they enjoy the sacrament talks, the activities, the camaraderie, and even see the fruits of the tree, but, like the Book of Mormon prophecy in which the people of the last days refuse any added scripture, say, "A bible, we have a Bible and we need no more" (2 Nephi 29:6). In so doing, they settle for less.

Life at this level is far greater and enriching than having no light at all. The light guides and comforts us when we are in need. It is wonderful. However, if we leave it at this, we cheat ourselves of the most rewarding part of the gospel while here on earth.

"These are they who receive of his glory, but not of his fullness. These are they who receive of the presence of the Son, but not of the fullness of the Father.... These are they who are not valiant in the testimony of Jesus; wherefore, they obtain not the crown over the kingdom of our God. Wherefore, they... differ in glory as the moon differs from the sun (D&C 76:76–79).

Here the valiant move ahead. They take the next step and "go forth and partake," even when they may not know why or what will be the end result. How did Lehi know the fruit would taste good or that it would not harm him? He willingly went forth, followed the path, and received the rewards of his efforts. "For he that diligently seeketh shall find; and the mysteries of God shall be unfolded unto them" (1 Nephi 10:19).

Perhaps the most challenging, yet most rewarding, experience in life is to first ask ourselves if, and then to conclude that, we are willing to pay the price to know and follow Christ. Only then will we experience the ultimate peace and joy this life can offer.

This Is Not an Overnight Process

Going forth on the path is a step-by-step process. "I will give unto the children of men line upon line, precept upon precept, here a little and there a little; and blessed are those who hearken unto my precepts, and lend an ear unto my counsel, for they shall learn wisdom; for unto him that receiveth I will give more" (2 Nephi 28:30).

These steps may not be what we expected and may even be the exact opposite of what we asked for. Individual steps may be different for each of us, though all lead to the same destination—peace in this life and eternal life with God. The key is asking God in prayer to help us determine our steps, and developing a relationship with the Spirit so we can have the guidance and faith to take them.

Four friends met through the singles program and instantly became close friends. For months, they enjoyed the laughter, deep and open talks, and great companionship. One evening after a singles dance, sitting in the foyer of the church and sharing their dance experiences, one challenged the others to return to the temple. None of them had current temple recommends, although three were returned missionaries. He encouraged the others to take that next step needed to reach such a goal. His challenge included meeting one day in the temple together.

That was their last meeting together as single friends. Soon one married and two started dating seriously. Nevertheless, all of them remembered their commitment made that night and knew what steps to take.

A year later, they met in the temple. What a joyous day! Feeling love and support from one another, each had grown in positive ways. Now with temple recommends, they committed to meet one day in the celestial kingdom, each with different steps to take to remain faithful, but each willing to do so.

This is merely an example of friends challenging one another to take the next step in their efforts to be more like God. We, like they, need to pray, ponder, and receive personal revelation so we can know our personal steps to grow closer to our Father in Heaven. Although these next steps may be different for all, let us look at what some of them might be.

Mending What Needs to Be Mended

One first step in following Christ and keeping His light in our lives is ridding ourselves of all that stands between God's light and us such as sin, pride, or fear.

Sin

Any act of sin, no matter the size, creates a barrier between God and us—a wall, as it were. Thus our access to God's spirit, light, and influence stops (see Alma 7:21). Sin literally separates us from God.

Now, God does not reject or desert us. In fact, the exact opposite occurs. By our choices, we leave and reject God. "For thus saith the Lord....To whom have I put thee away, or to which of my creditors have I sold you? Yea, to whom have I sold you? Behold, for your iniquities have ye sold yourselves" (Isaiah 50:1).

We know when we have the Spirit by the comfort, peace, and wholeness it brings. When the Spirits leaves us, that peace is interrupted—we feel empty, as if something is missing. Something *is* missing! This emptiness is an indicator, a built-in homing device that lets us know something needs to be changed. We need either to improve our relationship with our Father in Heaven or to take care of something amiss in our lives. "Yea, I say unto you come and fear not, and lay aside every sin which easily doth beset you, which doth bind you down to destruction" (Alma 7:25).

That "destruction" is our time away from the light. The more we yield to what separates us from God, the further away from the light we become and the less sensitive we are to the Spirit's influence. Left unchecked, it becomes almost impossible to know truth from error, light from darkness, and good from evil.

Pride

Pride is another barrier to light. "Are ye stripped of pride? I say unto you, if ye are not ye are not prepared to meet God" (Alma 5:28). Pride is a false sense of security, as it assumes we, or something else in this world, can do things as good or better than can God.

Our Father in Heaven often leaves us on our own when we are full of pride, as He did with the Nephites. "And because of this their great wickedness, and their boasting in their own strength, they were left in their own strength, therefore they did not prosper but were afflicted and smitten, and driven before the Lamanites, until they had lost possession of almost all their lands" (Helaman 4:13).

Jacob, the brother of Nephi, tells us, "Let not this pride of your hearts destroy your souls" (Jacob 2:16). When pride is in our hearts, there is potential for spiritual unraveling. We can end up questioning truth and developing a rebellious attitude. This does not happen overnight, but over time we create a wall which stops the flow of God's light into our souls.

You may ask, "How do I rid myself of pride?" The opposite of pride is humility, and, as Alma asks, "Could ye say, if ye were called to die at this time, within yourselves, that ye have been sufficiently humble? If ye are not, ye are not prepared to meet God" (Alma 5:28).

Humility acknowledges our limitations and the world's finite knowledge. Humility recognizes the power of the Savior, for without Him we could never reach perfection. With humility, we "hunger and thirst after righteousness" (Matthew 5:6). Humility helps us be what the Lord wants us to be, for "the Lord requires the heart and a willing mind" (D&C 64:34).

The Nephites teach us how to develop humility, "...they did fast and pray oft, and did wax stronger and stronger in their humility, and firmer and firmer in the faith of Christ, unto the filling their souls with joy and consolation...because of their yielding their hearts unto God" (Helaman 4:35). As we yield our hearts to God, we become more humble and more able to overcome our pride.

Fear

Fear is like placing a straightjacket on life. Moreover, unless we find a way around, over, or through it, we are bound, stifled, and unable to move and progress. Like placing a hand directly in front of our eyes, fear gets in the way of everything we need to see. Thus, fear holds us back, and can even hamper an open relationship with God.

Some people fear not finding the right relationship. Others fear facing life alone. Some fear the future, the unknown, or even success, while others are more afraid to live than to die.

Fear can lead us to sabotage the very things that mean the most. One friend told me that due to her fear of men, she gained weight so they would not notice her. We are told marriage will occur in the hereafter for those who do not marry in this life if it is due to no fault of their own. Could our fears—and our not growing beyond them—be our own fault? Might we be held accountable for those things we can change, but because of fear, we do not?

Some try to escape their fears by keeping busy, moving, seeking a new job, more money, or isolation. Not confronting our fears can lead to self-loathing and an inward spiral where we can become depressed, obsessed, addicted, or avoid what might lead us to happiness. Some people project their fear outwardly, where they attack, control, and get angry easily. Anger, jealousy, envy, resentment, abuse, greed, addiction, selfishness, and a need to control others are all expressions of fear.

As our path toward knowing God requires faith, growth, and movement, we then must rid ourselves of fear. "For God hath not given us the spirit of fear; but of power and of love, and of a sound mind" (2 Timothy 1:7). He goes on to say, "Fear thou not; for I am with thee: be not dismayed; for I am thy God: I will strengthen thee; yea, I will help thee; yea I will uphold thee with the right hand of my righteousness" (Isaiah 41:10). Oliver Cowdery was told, "Look unto me in every thought; doubt not, fear not" (D&C 6:36).

The scriptures also tell us, "perfect love casteth out fear." As we grow in God's love, our actions will sprout from that love. As we live our lives in a quest to love unconditionally, our love will conquer our fear, and a sense of peace will come into our lives.

Seeking Forgiveness and Forgiving

One of the early steps on the path to becoming Christlike is forgiving those who may have done us wrong and seeking forgiveness from anyone whom we might have offended.

A spirit of non-forgiveness toward anyone—the person in the apartment above who keeps doing their aerobics at 5 a.m. and waking us with their thundering thuds, or the person who left us alone and robbed us of the joys in life—can leave us bitter, angry, and hurt, all of which stop the Spirit from dwelling within us.

Ultimately, to have the Spirit's influence in our lives, we must forgive. Sometimes the only way we can do this is through prayer, pleading for help in forgiving just as Jesus forgave those who trespassed against Him. As we rise to become more like Christ and see through purer eyes, to love as He would love, we realize, as did the Savior, the offender's action comes out of fear, darkness, or even lack of understanding. The Savior meant it when He said, "Forgive them for they know not what they do." When we forgive another, the burden of their sin is lifted from our shoulders onto the shoulders of the Master, who said, "Take my yoke upon you .... and ye shall find rest unto your souls" (Matthew 11:29).

As much as we might be tempted to condemn, we are told to turn it over to God. "I, the Lord will forgive whom I will forgive, but of you it is required to forgive all men. And ye ought to say in your hearts—let God judge between me and thee, and reward thee according to thy deeds" (D&C 64:10–11). With the lack of forgiveness, just as with any other shortcoming, freedom occurs only when we yield our hearts to God.

But When It Is Really Bad

Some acts can be so hideous and mean we definitely feel justified in seeking revenge. Oh, that such events would not happen, but they do. God gave us our agency, and through the use of it, we have the right to make good and bad choices. This, unfortunately, means there will be victims. The focus of a victim may be different than that of others; his path requires he not only seek God in his life, but also includes healing, moving beyond, and forgiving.

You may want to say, "You just don't understand. I will never be able to forgive that person for what they did." You can choose that. However, as difficult as it seems to imagine letting go of such resentment, it is possible. For your mental, emotional, and spiritual health, it is critical.

When we don't forgive we close our hearts, and in doing so, we deny the flow of love. When we do not love, we close our hearts even to God's love. Perhaps that is why God said, "Wherefore, I say unto you that ye ought to forgive one another; for he that forgiveth not his brother his trespasses standeth condemned before the Lord; for there remaineth in him the greater sin" (D&C 64:9). Ultimately, our greatest pain comes from not experiencing God's love.

To keep our hearts open so we can love and be loved regardless of the actions of others requires forgiveness (see Matthew 5:44). It does not mean to live in denial or pretend everything is okay when it is not. Forgiveness is a soul-changing experience. It involves application of the Atonement (see chapter two) particularly when we cannot forgive on our own. When we give our shortcomings to the Savior, He will respond with His healing power. With His help, we can be filled with His love and the ability to truly forgive. In time, our hearts and souls will heal, and a sense of peace will return to our lives.

To Love as Jesus Loves

Another step on our path to be like Christ is to love as He loves. Paul reminds us, "Though I speak with the tongues of men and of angels, and have not charity, I am become as sounding brass, or a tinkling cymbal. And though I have the gift of prophecy, and understand all mysteries, and all knowledge; and though I have all faith, so that I could remove mountains, and have not charity, I am nothing" (1 Corinthians 13:1–2).

Charity is defined as the "pure love of Christ" (Moroni 7:47). If we do not have charity, to love as Jesus loves, in any and every situation, even when we do not want to, according to Paul, nothing else really matters.

No greater single attribute makes us more like the Savior than love. Thus, along our way, we must develop our ability to love as the Savior would love all men and women. The only way we develop such love is by allowing the Savior's love to penetrate our hearts. As His love fills us, we in turn love those around us, not because we feel obligated, but because there is an innate desire to go outside ourselves and be like Christ, to love like Christ. We see through His eyes that we each are children of God—not just when it is convenient or with those who are easy to love—but even with those who are needy, mean, or even hate us. Hence, we come to "always remember Him."

As an example, Mother Teresa once held a man on her lap who was dirty, smelly, starving, and oozing with sores. As she attempted to mend his wounds and give comfort, a cameraman from a television station asked how she could stand to hold such a dirty, smelly man. Revealing her complete dedication to serve the Savior and love as He would love, she smiled and said, "This is merely Jesus in disguise." Mother Teresa understood the pure love of Christ.

Jesus teaches us how to love in the scriptures. "A new

commandment I give unto you, That ye love one another; as I have loved you that ye also love one another" (John 13:34). His example of how to love follows: "For I was an hungred, and ye gave me meat: I was thirsty, and ye gave me drink: I was a stranger, and ye took me in: Naked, and ye clothed me: I was sick, and ye visited me: I was in prison, and ye came unto me. Then shall the righteous answer him, saying, Lord, when saw we thee an hungred, and fed thee? or thirsty, and gave thee drink…naked and clothed thee? Or when saw we thee sick, or in prison, and came unto thee?" And the Savior answered, "Verily I say unto you, Inasmuch as ye have done it unto one of the least of these my brethren, ye have done it unto me" (Matthew 25:35–40).

The Savior did not say to pretend or act as if you love, or love out of duty. He said love "as I have loved you." When we do acts of kindness from the pure love of Christ, we begin to understand what it means to be truly Christlike. He died and suffered for every lawbreaker, because He loved them and desired the best for them. He loved even those who betrayed and harmed Him. Loving even when we are rejected—is it anything short of what Jesus experienced? Should we try for anything less? "By this shall all men know that ye are my disciples, if ye have love one to another" (John 13:35).

Sacrifice

Sacrifice is another step often required of us when we choose to follow Christ. The ancient Israelites offered three kinds of sacrifices to God—a trespass offering, a burnt offering, and a peace offering.

With a trespass offering, the penitent gave the sacrificial animal over to the priest, and the animal became the property of the priest. This symbolized the handing over of our sins to God.

With a burnt offering, the offering was placed on the altar and burned completely through (see Leviticus 1:9) representing a total self-surrender to God.

For the peace offering, the priest prepared the animal carefully, apportioned some of the meat to the offerer to eat at a sacred feast. This ceremony symbolized the establishment of peace with God and hence, communion with God. (see Genesis 26:28–30; 31:44–54; and "Sacrifice in the Law of Moses," *Ensign*, Mar. 1990, 38–41).

When we hand over our sin to God, thus removing the barriers between God and us, and give our total selves completely to God, in essence we are then ready to experience the fifth road marker, peace and commune with God.

Lamoni's father, king over the Lamanites, understood the first level of sacrifice as he pleaded with God in prayer, "I will give away all my sins to know thee" (Alma 22:18).

None of us are without sin, hence, we all have sins to place on the altar. The real test comes in giving those that are not easy to give up. By placing every sin we have on the altar and loving God with all our might, mind, and soul, we will feel His presence in our lives and be able to experience that communion daily.

Giving Ourselves to God

"I would that you should come unto Christ…and offer your whole souls as an offering unto him" (Omni 1:26). Not just a part but our whole self—the good and the bad, the strong and the weak, the stress, the pain, the anger, the hurt, the whole, and all of its parts. And, not just on Sundays, but every day of our lives.

C. S. Lewis provides insight regarding the meaning of total self-sacrifice. "Christ says, 'Give me All. I don't want so much of your time and so much of your money and so much of your work: I want You.… I don't want to cut off a branch here and a branch there, I want to have the whole tree down— Hand over the whole natural self, all the desires which you think innocent as well as the ones you think wicked—the whole outfit. I will give you a new self instead. In fact, I will give you Myself: my own will shall become yours.'"[1]

Neal A. Maxwell adds:

> There can be no conditions attached to unconditional surrender to God. Unconditional surrender means we can not keep our obsessions, possessions, or cheering constituencies. Even our customized security blankets must go.
>
> Does this sound too severe and too sacrificing? If so, it is only until we realize that if we yield to Him, He will give us everything He has (D&C 84:38). Anyone, for example, who prepares to sit down at that culminating banquet with Jesus, Abraham, Isaac, and Jacob, certainly would not bring along his own beef jerky. Nor would he send an advance press agent to tout his accomplishments to that special company and in the presence of Him who trod the winepress alone (D&C 76:107).
>
> Our personal trinkets, if carried even that far, are to be left outside at the doorstep or in the courtyard, where such clutter and debris would indicate the shedding of selfishness.[2]

Some of us refuse to give our whole selves over to God. We want to hold onto some resentment, carnal desire, or irritation, and believe by so doing we can keep some control. But Mosiah tells us to become "as a child, submissive...,willing to submit to all things which the lord seeth fit to inflict upon him even as a child doth submit to his father" (Mosiah 3:19). Then he adds, "Submit cheerfully and with patience to all the will of the Lord" (Mosiah 24:15). For "the Lord requireth the heart and a willing mind" (D&C 64:34).

In today's world many consider it unfashionable to be submissive to God, but Paul declared in 1 Corinthians 7:31, "The fashions of this world passeth away." "Letting go and letting God" means we recognize that in order to achieve true peace and joy, we must surrender the control, the forcing, the egotism, and allow our Heavenly Father to take charge. This requires faith and trust that He knows what He is doing, and faith in Him to follow His lead, be it in our parenting, in relationships and in all that we do.

We say, "God, I trust thee and thy will. And though I may not know the end result, I leave it all in thine hands because I know it will be for good."

It Is a Process

If giving our whole self to God seems overwhelming, then let us start by offering to God our "I don't know what to do with my life" dilemma. Neal Maxwell suggests, "In this dispensation what we place on the altar is not an animal but the animal in us."[3] So let's begin by placing the animal in us on the altar, then listen to and follow the promptings of the Spirit for our next step. Soon we will find courage and increased understanding, and a greater ability to offer the good, then the bad, and then the whole, natural self.

President Kimball said, "We must sacrifice whatever is required by the Lord. We begin by offering a 'broken heart and contrite spirit.' We follow this by giving our best effort in our assigned fields of labor and in our callings. We learn our duty and execute it fully. Finally we consecrate our time, talents, and means as called upon by our file leaders and as prompted by the whisperings of the Spirit."[4] The bottom line is that we are given a self so that we can sacrifice it.

This does not mean we sit back and wait for our Father in Heaven to do the work. God gave us talents in this life so that we might improve and contribute to the building of His kingdom. By submitting our lives and talents to Him, we accomplish far more than we ever would on our own.

President Ezra Taft Benson once said, "Men and women who turn their lives over to God will find out that He can make a lot more out of their lives than they can. He will deepen their joys, expand their vision, quicken their minds, strengthen their muscles, lift their spirits, multiply their blessings, increase their opportunities, comfort their souls, raise up friends, and pour out peace. Whoever will lose his life to God will find he has eternal life."[5]

Holding on to an eternal perspective—realizing our spiritual being is of permanent status, and our mortal self is but temporary—helps us look beyond the matters of this world and makes it easier to surrender to the laws of God. As we realize God's greatness, that He knows all, including what is best for us, we can give Him our fears and follow His lead.

Jesus, who served the best of all and experienced the worst of all, gave the greatest example of submission when He asked God for the bitter cup to be removed. Oh Father, I would rather not do what thou art asking—to suffer and die. Yet the Savior ended His prayer with, "Nevertheless not my will but as thou wilt" (Matthew 26:39) and gave Himself and His mortal life as a ransom for all of us. The ultimate example of sacrifice!

Enduring

Let us say we have taken all the steps shown us. The ultimate test now is enduring to the end, no matter what, no matter where, no matter when, and no matter how long. The Savior says, "Look to me, and endure to the end...for unto him that endureth to the end will I give eternal life" (3 Nephi 15:9). Alma tells his son Shiblon, "For blessed is he that endureth to the end" (2 Nephi 38:2).

The word "endure" implies that the path will not be easy, and in some cases, will be long. It means staying committed to the Savor and his plan, to the end. Nephi, in his parting testimony said, "Be reconciled unto Christ, and enter into the narrow gate, and walk in the straight path which leads to life, and continue in the path until the end" (2 Nephi 33:9).

You see, the difference between Satan and ourselves is not what we know about God. Satan may know more about God than we do, but just knowing and believing won't make the grade. The difference is our commitment to follow God no matter what, no matter how long, and no matter the conditions.

I think of Job's faithfulness when under extreme adversity. He was one of the greatest, most respected, and wealthy men of his time, but still praised God when he lost his wealth, "The Lord gave, and the Lord hath taken away; blessed be the name of the LORD" (Job 1:22). Then Satan inflicted Job with sore boils that so disfigured his face that none of his friends could recognize him. Maggots bred in his sores and so terrible was the pain that Job's wife tried to get him to "curse God and die." But Job replied to her, "Shall we receive good at the hand of God, and shall we not receive evil?" (Job 2:10).

Where once he was honored by the noble, he now lived on the outskirts of town and was abused by the lowest of life. In his deepest moments of need, Job stood alone "abhorred" by his friends, abandoned by his family. "They whom I loved are turned against me" (Job 19:13–22). Even God remained silent to Job's continual question of *Why?* "Behold, I cry out of wrong, but I am not heard.... He hath fenced up my way that I cannot pass, and he hath set darkness in my paths" (Job 19:6–8). "Oh that I knew where I might find him!" (Job 23:3). Job even longed for death (see Job 6:8–11), but he never deviated from his course, knowing he was pursuing the course pleasing to God. He willingly followed God no matter the conditions, even when he did not understand. Job expressed the ultimate commitment in following God when he

said, "Though he slay me, Yet will I trust in him: My righteousness
I hold fast, and will not let it go...so long as I live" (Job 27:2–6;
31).

Are we willing to trust and commit to God like Job, or like
the pioneers whose conditions took many of them to their death,
without "charging God foolishly" (Job 1:22)? If conditions required us to sacrifice even to death, would we cave in and say
to God, "Oh, I was just kidding. I really didn't want to take this
ride!"?

Sometimes living for the gospel is tougher than dying for it.
We often do not understand the eternal perspective, as the rich
man in this parable:

> There was a certain rich man, which was clothed in purple
> and fine linen, and fared sumptuously every day;
> And there was a certain beggar named Lazarus, which was
> laid at his gate full of sores,
> And desiring to be fed with the crumbs which fell from the
> rich man's table: moreover the dogs came and licked his sores.
> And it came to pass, that the beggar died, and was carried
> by the angels into Abraham's bosom: the rich man also died,
> and was buried;
> And in hell he lift up his eyes, being in torments, and seeth
> Abraham afar off, and Lazarus in his bosom.
> And he cried and said, Father Abraham, have mercy on me,
> and send Lazarus, that he may dip the tip of his finger in water,
> and cool my tongue; for I am tormented in this flame.
> But Abraham said, Son, remember that thou in thy lifetime
> receivedst thy good things, and likewise Lazarus evil things:
> but now he is comforted, and thou art tormented. [Luke
> 16:19–25]

We cannot imagine what glory awaits those who endure that
which is given to them in this life. We are promised if we endure

well, we will live with our Father in Heaven. "Look unto me, and endure to the end, and ye shall live; for unto him that endureth to the end will I give eternal life" (3 Nephi 15:9).

Notes

1. C. S. Lewis, *Mere Christianity*, 1996, 167—copyright © C.S. Lewis Pte. Ltd. 1942, 1943, 1944, 1952.

2. Neal A. Maxwell, *Not My Will, But Thine*, 1988, 92–93.

3. Ibid.

4. Spencer W. Kimball, "Becoming the Pure in Heart," *Ensign,* March 1985, 5.

5. Ezra Taft Benson, "Jesus Christ—Gifts and Expectations," *Ensign,* December 1988, 20.

Chapter Nine

OUR SOUL IS FILLED

WOW! WHAT A PATH! In deciding to follow Christ, we experience darkness, pray for God's mercy, and receive His light. Then we take the steps shown us by that light, all the while attempting to endure to the end. Now you may ask, "What's it all for? Is it really worth it? It seems like so much work."

If you recall, after Lehi takes the steps illuminated before him, he reaches the "tree of life" and tastes its fruit. He describes his experience: "I beheld that it was the most sweet, above all that I ever before tasted. Yea and...white, to exceed all the whiteness that I had ever seen. And as I partook of the fruit thereof it filled my soul with exceeding great joy" (1 Nephi 8:11–12). Lehi experienced the effects of the fruit of the "tree of life," the essence of what life is all about, and was filled with God's love. This is our road marker five—our soul is filled.

I ask what I asked earlier, "Do you know what he is talking about? Have you ever experienced what Lehi describes?" Have you been so filled with God's love that you experienced "exceeding great joy" in your soul?

You might say, "It's impossible to feel such a level of joy in this life. Life is just too difficult and complicated. Besides, it takes too much effort."

Joanie knew what Lehi talked about. Before her death, while fighting cancer, she penned Joanie's Prayer. "Pain, suffering, fear, these are not things of God. They are, however, realities of life. When you face these realities and accept them as challenges and opportunities, even though they seem unfair or unjust, then the realities of God: joy, peace, fulfillment, come to you almost to the point of feeling overwhelmed. The trick is to work with God and surrender to his will. After that, the fun begins!"[1]

No other happiness, no other material possession, no other relationship creates the joy, peace, and fulfillment that a life centered on Christ and submitting to His will brings. The Savior said, "I will impart unto you of my Spirit,... which shall fill your soul with joy" that "thou mayest know the mysteries and peaceable things—that which brings joy" (D&C 11:13; 42:61).

Peace comes as we live in harmony with truth and experience the fruit of God's love, no matter the circumstances. We can talk about it and have glimpses of it, but until we go through the process to come to know God and His love, we will never understand what Lehi talked about when he described being filled with "exceeding great joy."

You see, once we are filled with God's love, material things and life circumstances are not so important. We can be rich or poor, loved by all or not so many, tired or rested, married or single, or alone or with children. These things no longer consume us. We may desire them, but even without them we are filled with love and the peaceable things not of this world.

We become balanced, enlightened, and in harmony with God because we are truly one with Him and His Son. "That I may be in them as thou, Father, art in me, that we may be one" (3 Nephi 19:23; see John 17:22).

Explaining in more detail, the Savior said, "... that they may be one, even as we are one... that they may be made perfect in one; and that the world may know that thou... hast loved them, as thou hast loved me... that the love wherewith thou hast loved me may be in them, and I in them" (John 17:21–23, 26). No greater, more perfect love, and no greater sense of wholeness exists than when we incorporate God's love into our lives and become one with Him. That love softens us and we are gentle and kind. Any other fulfillment is only temporary and will leave us yearning for something more.

In addition, when we are where we are supposed to be and doing what we are supposed to do, no matter the adversity, we can feel confidence and joy and a sweet assurance that we are on the right path. "He who doeth the works of righteousness shall receive his reward, even peace in this world" (D&C 59:23). In essence, we are filling the measure of our creation.

Nephi knew what this fulfillment is like. "He hath filled me with his love, even unto the consuming of my flesh" (2 Nephi 4:21), describing it as "the most desirable above all things... and the most joy unto the soul" (1 Nephi 11:22–23). Ammon exclaimed, "Behold, my joy is full, yea my heart is brim with joy, and I will rejoice in my God" (Alma 26:11).

Enoch and his people followed these road markers and understood communing and union with God. "And Enoch and all his people walked with God" (Moses 7:69), and God called them the "City of Holiness, even Zion" (Moses 7:19). "And the Lord called his people Zion, because they were of one heart and one mind, and dwelt in righteousness" (Moses 7:18). Because of their righteousness, "Zion was taken up into heaven" and Enoch was "lifted up, even in the bosom of the Father, and of the Son of Man (Moses 7:23–24). Imagine our whole community living on this level, one with God, together.

An interesting note about Lehi's dream is that Lehi was alone every step of the way. In his dream, the Savior came to Lehi—one-on-one—and invited him, alone, to follow. Lehi experienced the darkness alone; his plea for mercy and receiving God's light was one-on-one. Lehi partook and tasted the fruit of the tree, God's love, by himself. He was alone when he experienced the sweetness and purity of God's love.

No one else could have experienced it for him. As in our lives, others may help in the process, but no matter if we are married or single, have a family or live alone, ultimately coming to know God, experiencing a change of heart, being filled with God's love is, for all of us, a one-on-one, singular, and individual experience.

Only after Lehi experienced the "path" alone did he turn to his loved ones to share his joy and God's love. A characteristic of knowing God is that we shift from self-centered living to Christ-centered living. We desire to share with others the truth, love, joy, and peace, we know.

Alma reminds us of another important point as he asks, "Have [you] felt to sing the song of redeeming love," and continues, if so, "can you feel so now?" (Alma 5:26). Like the Israelites who gathered manna daily, if it were saved, it would spoil—so it is with our spirituality. It is a daily process, needing daily contributions. "If ye have known of his goodness and have tasted of his love, and have received a remission of your sins which causeth such exceeding great joy in your souls, even so I would that ye should remember, and always retain in remembrance, the greatness of God and humble yourselves, calling on him daily, and standing steadfast in the faith and…if ye do this ye shall always rejoice and be filled with the love of God" (Mosiah 4:11–12).

We can, if we choose to, grovel in darkness the rest of our days, piling up issues, creating a life more and more complicated and out of control and just accept this as life. Perhaps this way may be easier and even fun initially, but such behavior will never release us from life's dilemmas, nor will it allow us to taste the sweetness which could be ours. Alternatively, we can turn to God, follow His lead, and receive the peace and fulfillment we long for here and now during our life on earth. The choice is up to each one of us. Oh, the greatness of God and, oh, the joy that awaits those who are willing to pay the price!

God promises that those who love and follow Him will inherit His kingdom, "eye hath not seen, nor ear heard, the things He has prepared for them" (see Corinthians 2:9), where we will "dwell in the presence of God and our Lord, Jesus Christ forever (D&C 76:62). Not only is it worth waiting for, it is worth *living* for!

Notes

1. Joan Gibson, May 1991.

Part Three
THE CHALLENGE

Chapter Ten

THE BATTLE

THIS IS WAR! ALL-OUT WAR! The battles wage and it's anyone's guess as to who will win. This war does not take mortal lives, nor is the battle over who has the better idea. On the contrary, this is a war that started long before this world began (see Revelation 12:7–9)—between good and evil, light and darkness, truth and error, happiness versus pain, following or denying Christ. This war threatens so many of our spiritual lives, the consequences of which far out reach the loss of our mortal existence. The casualties have been great, and, much to our chagrin, it is not likely to end soon.

Perhaps the biggest battle we face in this great war is within the chambers of our own souls as we attempt to establish and maintain the inner peace that a life centered on Christ brings. We develop that peace by following the path the Savior created. But, what about the forces fighting to prevent us from having that experience?

Satan and his followers are out to destroy our peace. They take great pleasure in manipulating us until we ultimately question the

Savior's path. Satan never explains where his path leads—trapped, addicted, and obsessed, in constant search of immediate gratification, only to be left empty in the end.

Satan would have us believe that the only route to true joy is through self-gratification. With pleasure, we may feel whole or complete for a moment, but as with every other counterfeit ploy Satan uses, it is not real and it will not last. Our yearning for more continues.

In fact, this is how Satan traps us. Like an addict who gives up experiencing life chasing that ultimate "high," we cling to worldly pleasures in an effort to fill the void within us. Then, blinded by those cravings and because of the fear of letting go and acknowledging the emptiness within, our compulsive pleasure-seeking and pain-avoidance takes over, allowing our souls to decay.

Once caught in the gratification cycle, Satan's work is done, because at this point, our own habits and addictions keep us trapped. "Every man is tempted, when he is drawn away of his own lust, and enticed. Then when lust hath conceived, it bringeth forth sin: and sin, when finished, bringeth forth death" (James 1:14–15).

We need no pills or razor blades to end our lives because addiction to gratification helps us commit a slow spiritual suicide—first by deadening our feelings and talents, then by leading us on a downward spiral of self-defeating behaviors. With enough time, every aspect of our personalities, spirit, and even our bodies can end up destroyed. "Remember to be carnally-minded is death, and to be spiritually-minded is life eternal" (2 Nephi 9:39).

Following the plan of the Savior does not mean that we should not enjoy life. In fact, "men are, that they might have joy" (2 Nephi 2:25). Joseph Smith reminds us, "Happiness is the object and design of our existence; and will be the end thereof, if we pursue the path that leads to it; and this path is virtue, uprightness, faithfulness, holiness, and keeping all the commandments of

God."[1] Real joy and contentment come when we follow the path of righteousness.

We must be clear about the difference between joy and pleasure. Pleasure is a temporary state and fills us for the moment. Joy goes beyond the moment, even into the eternities. Ask these three questions: "Is what I am seeking at the moment leading me closer to what I want in the end? Will this moment bring joy to my life once the moment is over?" And, "Will this moment enhance my life in a pleasing way to God?"

If we can answer "yes" to all of the above, then that moment becomes another drop in our buckets of true joy. And when our life on earth is complete, we can look on these moments with feelings of fulfillment and a depth of joy insurmountable when compared to any moment of pleasure.

But what a battle in sacrificing the immediate for something we cannot see—the long-term glory and peace, life eternal, and the kind of joy only Christ can bring. The other side looks so inviting, and oh, how we sometimes want to let go and simply indulge. Sometimes following the path and enduring is so difficult. What is it all for anyway? Does it really matter? Won't we be hit with just a "few stripes" (see 2 Nephi 28:8), and then it will all be better?

Not only does Satan desire to capture us so we become as miserable as he is—"…men are free according to the flesh; and they are free to choose liberty and eternal life, through the great mediation of all men, or to choose captivity and death, according to the captivity and power of the devil; for he seeketh that all men might be miserable like unto himself" (2 Nephi 2:27)—but he desires to control and destroy the world. As more and more individuals seek gratification of their immediate pleasure and selfish desires, more and more conflicts occur. The more selfishness, the greater the conflicts, and the greater is Satan's hold.

However, if each of us experiences peace in our own souls, that peace would be reflected in our relationships and eventually spread throughout the land and, indeed, the world. As the Savior announced, "I bring you good tidings of great joy" (Luke 2:10). Imagine how it would be if we had no more violence and misuse of each other, but, on the contrary, a world of peace. Imagine the joy we would experience. So, why don't we all live to have that happen?

So How Did This Battle Start?

In the premortal battle—the War in Heaven—(see Revelation 12:7–9), Satan proposed a plan that he said would ensure us all a return ticket home after this mortal existence (see Moses 4:1). His plan required nothing from us—no agency to choose good or evil. Yet, in the end, he said that we would get what we wanted—life eternal with our Father in Heaven. No one would be lost. Everyone that we love would be there.

The Savior, on the other hand, supported the plan of the Father, giving us our own choice, requiring work, pain, responsibility, and accountability. It was not the easier way. In fact, many would get lost along the way. We would return to live with our Father in Heaven only if we followed the designated path.

Now here on earth, fighting the pressures of the world and feeling battle-fatigued, we may wonder why we didn't go for Lucifer's plan—just sit back and let someone else make the decisions. "I don't want to *think* any more, I don't want to *do* anymore."

Maybe the third of the hosts of heaven who followed Lucifer believed they could have ensured victory—all back together in the end with God. Maybe they thought it would be worth the frustration of a little "forced righteousness" thus guaranteeing the automatic return to live with God. Although there would be no growth because there would be no pain in this life, to them the plan must have sounded good.

Perhaps the Savior's plan might have sounded a little irrespon-sible by seemingly allowing everyone to do what they wanted and then to wait and see what would happen. Didn't God, our Father in Heaven, care more about us than to just let us make decisions that might jeopardize our return to Him? Why wouldn't He set a plan with a guarantee like Satan did? Didn't He want us back with Him again?

So why *did* we choose the Savior's plan? What made us see beyond merely our return home to God?

The significant difference between Lucifer's plan and the Fa-ther's, which was led by Jesus, was one of agency—freedom to choose righteousness or evil. It would be up to us. Through our choices, we would experience suffering and pain, as well as peace and joy. Through the process, we would have opportunities to grow in understanding and be more like our Father in Heaven.

Did we really understand the eternal significance of what our choice at that time would mean? Did we really understand the significance of this earthly experience, putting our eternal pro-gression, eternal character, and lives on the line? Did we know the pain and human misery that choosing the Savior's plan would bring? Would it have mattered if we had known?

How fortunate we are that this plan was decided upon and implemented. Sometimes we need an eternal perspective so we can truly appreciate this wonderful gift when life seems so endless and the freedom to choose seems too hard. But what growth and understanding we gain through the hard times!

What about Agency?

So why is agency such an important element in this plan? What did agency offer us that Lucifer's plan did not?

Using our agency, we grow as we learn from consequences—the fruits of our labor—that what we sow is what we reap. We develop understanding as we experience pain and suffering, not just from our own use of agency but also from that of everyone else. We develop character as we realize not even God will interfere with our right to choose nor will He force anyone to do good.

You see, it is a given that we all will be saved from the bands of death; that is, we will all be resurrected because of the Savior's atoning sacrifice. But the whole premise of agency is our ability to choose our ultimate and eternal destination—that of returning home to be with God or not! In fact, through our agency, we have the power to choose the city, town, and country and perhaps even the block and size of mansion we want, as it were, when we return to heaven. And because we each have control over that outcome and we have our agency, we have no one to blame, other than ourselves, not even God, for the outcome.

The reality is that we can live any way we desire, but God has set the consequences of our actions. Even if we do not see them in this life, consequences are there and we will see them in the life to come.

Does this sound like a raw deal to be making choices but not choosing the consequences? The plan was designed for us to develop and grow beyond our natural selves, to develop integrity, discipline, and understanding beyond our own selfishness and passions—ultimately to build Christ-like character. Without the choices and battles that come with our agency, these qualities would never be ours.

Other realities we face are the intrusions and suffering because of another's agency. We can become innocent victims of deviant behaviors, crime, and immorality.

We accepted wickedness as inevitable in this life full of opposition and chose to face it when we agreed upon the plan. We were prepared to suffer the bad with the good for the right to live in a world of agency, full of autonomous beings.

When we came here to earth, we knew there would be risks. However, I think we were excited about this plan because we knew we could rise above the occasion and meet the challenge. We had confidence that we would make the choices that would guarantee us eternal life with our Father in Heaven. I think we were excited for the opportunity to grow and show God we could do it—to show Him our love and devotion, that we would follow Him no matter what, despite the opposition.

Back to Earth

Now, the mere fact that we are here on earth lets us know which way we voted in the premortal existence. Lucifer and his followers were cast out of the heavens when they rebelled against the Father's plan. They now reside in spirit form, all around us, trying to foil the plan of salvation and our chances to reap the rewards of following that plan. Their sole task is winning over as many as they can who voted against their god, Lucifer. The battle is real. Satan is real, and his cause is going forward in full force (see D&C 50:2–3). The fact that we are living here on earth means that we are already drafted into the forces, into the battle. How we fight, how long we fight, and for what we fight are what is in question.

How Satan Works—What the Battle Looks Like

No longer is this a "gentlemen's war." We are now in "jungle warfare" where anything goes. And anything does go when it comes to how Satan and his angels attempt to snare us into their hold.

You see, Satan knows his power to destroy is heightened if he can separate us from the Light and Spirit of God. Just as wolves will separate one sheep from the rest for the kill, Satan will separate us from the fold, away from the protective care of truth and light. Once vulnerable and unable to fight back, he then attacks.

But while Satan's approach is initially very subtle and slow moving, he strikes at the roots of our emotional, social, physical, and spiritual well-being. Left unchecked, more roots are cut and, like a tree, more branches grow bare. With enough roots severed, the tree, too weak to bear growth, fruit, and leaves, is left barren to die. And oh, how Satan and his forces celebrate the victory!

Of course, none of us would say explicitly that we follow Satan, but many of us are lured, either through indifference or choice, by the subtle enticing of his spirit. We see his influence on television in movies, music, and in our everyday experiences with others. He has done a great job making good look bad, and bad look good, convincing us that indulging in the carnal pleasures will fill any void we may have.

Simple selfishness is a start down his path. He never bothers to tell us that the only true sense of joy and happiness comes by living the physical, intellectual, and spiritual laws of God. "Wickedness never was happiness" (Alma 41:10). Going against these laws brings imbalance and unhappiness into our lives. Thus, to have peace and joy, we must live the laws upon which they are predicated.

Consider the analogy of the ship out at sea. With the slightest change in the rudder, mere inches initially, a planned destination can be missed by miles. Thus, not only by small and simple things do great things come to pass for good, but so too with evil. Small, seemingly insignificant choices in the beginning can create major negative shifts and even possible destruction in the end. As a great writer once said, "Hell is giving up what we want most for that which we want now."

How Satan Distorts

People who live close to the Spirit will experience a sense of loss and emptiness after an initial bout with carnal pleasure, evil, or sin. It will feel like a hole in their souls, like something is missing. Something *is* missing—the Spirit of God. As light and darkness cannot dwell in the same place at the same time (see 1 John 1:5), the Spirit leaves when darkness enters. When the Spirit leaves, it is like the loss of a good friend; we feel empty.

This uneasiness is God-given, letting us know something in our lives is in disharmony. Without heeding the emptiness as a warning signal, we soon forget what it is like to live harmoniously and at one with the Spirit. With time, we may dangerously conclude that the dissonance is just normal, and thus the distortion begins.

Let us look at some ways Satan sets the wedge and distorts.

Discouragement

Satan tries to undermine and discourage us at any point he can and takes advantage of our down moments. For example, Satan uses discord and turns it into discouragement, prompting us to think thoughts such as: "I am so bad" and "God must really not care about me." Satan wants us to think, "Don't try" or "Why try?" thus convincing us to surrender to our passions and give up.

Satan discourages singles by planting thoughts such as, "They don't really care," or, "I'd never fit in," or even, "They just do not understand me and my situation." He distorts our perspective regarding the Church, "I can never be as good as everyone else," or, "I cannot live the way the Church expects me to." As a result of his influence, we may stop attending church. "Why hath Satan got such great hold upon your hearts? Why will ye yield yourselves unto him that he might have power over you, to blind your eyes, that ye will not understand the words which are spoken according to their faith?" (Alma 10:25).

Satan's discouragement makes us feel as if there is no escape, no relief or hope in sight. We feel overpowering darkness, as if the walls are falling in all around us. He would have us believe that we are alone, that no one cares, and that we have no way out. He would have us think we are evil when we are not, and then cause us to despise and turn against ourselves. He has succeeded in convincing many that they are not loved or wanted.

If we ever have such ideas we must break through them by praying and asking for God's mercy, love, and the light of His understanding. If He does not intercede at that moment, He will lead us to those who can comfort and help. As we trust God and pray for His intervention, Satan will lose his power and influence and we will feel God's comforting presence again.

Guilt

Guilt is a gift from God and lets us know when we have done something that offends the Spirit. Guilt, when used by the Spirit, is Godly sorrow. As a result we desire to follow God's word and come closer to Him. We are remorseful and desire to repent.

Satan distorts guilt. He tries to move us away from God, convincing us that we are unworthy of God's forgiveness and His love. Satan wants us to believe that God would never forgive us. Under Satan's influence, depression, self-destruction, and discouragement set in and we are taken further from God. On the contrary, guilt under the influence of the Spirit creates a desire to draw closer to God and to do whatever is necessary to remove any barriers that stand in the way of our relationship with God.

Satan plays head-games with the single individual, especially when it comes to dating and morality. He tries to convince us how impossible dating is without immorality and will tempt us to commit indiscretions. Then when we're spiritually vulnerable, he keeps us under his power by using his awful form of guilt and discouragement, initiating thoughts such as: "Why try," or "Why not just give in?" or "Everybody else in the world is doing it. Besides, I can't do what God is asking of me."

Knowing that God asks us to be morally straight lets us know we can win this battle just as in Nephi's exclamation which follows: "The Lord giveth no commandments unto the children of men, save he shall prepare a way for them that they may accomplish the thing which he commandeth them" (1 Nephi 3:7). We can date in a manner pleasing to God and avoid morality problems through the power of His influence. As Nephi tells us, God will provide a way for us to be obedient.

I am convinced that one of the greatest battles that builds Christlike character for singles is overcoming and enduring the battle for morality. Working in concert with God, we find ways to accomplish that which He asks. As we seek our Father in Heaven's love and regain and maintain the Spirit's influence in our lives, we will have the peaceful harmony the Spirit brings and the power to resist Satan's fiery darts.

Getting Stuck

Satan wants us stuck. He wants us to fail our trials and will do whatever it takes to get us to cave in. There is no growth if we do not get back up and try again. In fact, each step closer to Christ is a step more purified and sanctified, and exactly what Satan does not want. If he can discourage us and stop the process, he not only halts our progression toward eternal life, but, in his mind, comes closer to foiling God's overall plan.

Counterfeits and Deceit

As we have mentioned, Satan counterfeits true joy and peace when we indulge in carnal pleasures. When we flirt with temptation, thinking we can handle it, or begin rationalizing our behaviors, we are being influenced by Satan's distortions. He distorts our thinking by using justification and rationalization, even leading us to think that the Church leaders are too old or out of touch with reality. We may begin to feel restricted by the "rules of an out-dated Church."

Once a wedge is set, Satan then places false gods before us, distracting us from God Himself. These false gods can be a person or our personal gains, fears, obsessions, passions, anger, knowledge, intellect, bottles of wine, drugs, food, or even ourselves. The more distracted we are by the things of the world, the more likely we will develop allegiance to them, and, in a sense, worship them.

The Inner Battle—the Split Within

Joshua said, "As for me and my house we will serve the Lord" (Joshua 24:15). Perhaps we can look at our own inner house and determine if we are serving God. Not just a part, but are all parts of ourselves following and serving the Lord? A perfect example of this is Adam's son, Cain. According to scripture, it was not that Cain did not love God but that he loved earthly gains more (see Genesis 4:1–16). The result was that he killed his brother Abel.

Whom, or what, do we love more? Where is our allegiance? Do we worship God on Sundays, but on Friday and Saturday nights worship those things authored by Satan? Can we tell by the fruits of our actions where we place out trust?

Perhaps a part of us is not quite committed to following the path the Savior has set. Perhaps a part us is still greedy, angry, resentful, proud, selfish, and desires worldly pleasures before seeking God. We say we love God, but if we do not bring the undermining parts of ourselves into the fold, we are a "house divided."

The Savior said, "No man can serve two masters: for either he will hate the one, and love the other; or else he will hold to the one, and despise the other. Ye cannot serve God and mammon" (Matthew 6:24). This split leads to conflict and confusion. Unchanged, it results in misery and even potential spiritual death.

The conflict is between the flesh and the spirit. The flesh, or the body, is by nature an enemy to God. "For the natural man is an enemy to God, and has been from the fall of Adam, and will be, forever and ever, unless he yields to the enticings of the Holy Spirit, and putteth off the natural man and becometh a saint through the atonement of Christ the Lord" (Mosiah 3:19).

The flesh cannot distinguish between good and evil and only registers what is pleasurable and what is painful. Thus, the drive of the flesh is to seek pleasure and avoid pain. Life teaches us succinctly the sorrows we reap from letting the flesh take charge.

On the other hand, the spirit part of ourselves distinguishes truth and error, light and darkness. It comprehends which desires of the body will be self-destructive and which will enhance our lives. Our spirit understands the long-term needs of the soul and what in the present will fill those needs. The tough part is being able to hear that very soft voice, guiding and directing us, versus the loud, self-indulging voice of the flesh that cries as a spoiled child wanting its way.

Many of us do not trust what we cannot see—things of the spirit. Instead, we trust what can be seen, that which is of the arm of flesh. But Alma warns us and gives us insight on this bondage when he explains to his son Corianton, "And now, my son, all men that are in a state of nature, or I would say, in a carnal state, are in the gall of bitterness and in the bonds of iniquity; they are without God in the world, and they have gone contrary to the nature of God; therefore, they are in a state contrary to the nature of happiness" (Alma 41:11).

If left unchecked, the flesh will seek self-pleasure even to the point of self-destruction. However, our Father in Heaven has given us checks and balances to prevent this by allowing our spirits to be influenced by the promptings of the Holy Ghost. As we listen and comply with these promptings, our physical self aligns with our spiritual self and, as both submit to God, true harmony of being begins. We then experience integrity, character, and one-ness with self.

Submitting to God becomes easier as we discipline the temporal and feed the spiritual. Each time we follow God's will we grow. We feel a sense of integrity. We become more disciplined, more noble in character and self-respect, more self-confident, more aware of others, and more in-tune with the Spirit. Most importantly, we grow closer to God. Thus, our sensitivity to the Spirit and our ability to follow Him increases.

But Satan Is Powerful

Describing the wickedness of ancient America, Ether says, "Behold, the Spirit of the Lord had ceased striving with them, and Satan had full power over the hearts of the people; for they were given up unto the hardness of their hearts, and the blindness of their minds" (Ether 15:19).

When we are away from the Spirit for extended periods of time, we can become "hard-hearted" or as the scriptures tell us, "beyond feeling." "Thou knowest the wickedness of this people; thou knowest that they are without principle, and past feeling" (Moroni 9:20).

Truth offends the hard-hearted. They become defensive and prideful, often convincing others that their way is better. Speaking of the Nephites, Mormon says, "And when I speak the word of God with sharpness they tremble and anger against me; and when I use no sharpness they harden their hearts against it; wherefore, I fear lest the Spirit of the Lord hath ceased striving with them" (Moroni 9:4).

When someone decides to indulge for a time in the pleasures of the world, and says that afterward they will repent, they often never come back. They don't because: 1) it is tough letting go once the flesh gets caught up in the pleasures of sin, greed, selfishness, and the narrow-mindedness that following the flesh brings; 2) they become more self-centered as they focus on their carnal desires, away from God; and 3) the more they indulge that part of themselves, the less appealing spiritual things are, and, with time, they lose interest in developing the spiritual self.

Letting the Spirit lead allows for both pleasure and joy, giving us an awareness that there is a time and season for everything (see Ecclesiastes 3:1). Every healthy part of us will be expressed and fulfilled as we develop, trust, and let the Spirit lead. The Spirit knows when and how to orchestrate our lives to meet all of our needs.

Nevertheless, even if we lose some of the battles, remember that the war is not over. The key is to get back up, brush ourselves off and engage back into the battle. As we develop spiritual strength, we will gain the light and understanding to know what really matters. We will find the peace, truth, and joy that come from knowing God's love. As we stay within the fold, so we will have the necessary support to remain faithful and endure.

Notes

1. *History of the Church*, 5:134–35.

Chapter Eleven

RESISTING THE DEVIL

WE ARE ADMONISHED to put on the armor of God. "Wherefore, lift up your hearts and rejoice, and gird up your loins, and take upon you my whole armor, that ye may be able to withstand the evil day.... Stand, therefore, having your loins girt about with truth, having on the breastplate of righteousness, and your feet shod with the preparation of the gospel of peace, which I have sent mine angels to commit unto you; taking the shield of faith wherewith ye shall be able to quench all the fiery darts of the wicked; and take the helmet of salvation, and the sword of my Spirit,...and be faithful until I come, and ye shall be caught up, that where I am ye shall be also" (D&C 27:15–18).

We must put on the whole armor of God in our efforts to resist the adversary. But how exactly do we do this? How do we build such armor and shield ourselves in a world consumed by evil?

James tells us if we "submit to God" and "resist the devil...he [the devil] will flee from [us]" (James 4:7). We have already discussed ways we can submit to God, but how do we resist the devil to the point that he flees? How do we ensure victory in this great battle over evil?

How to Resist the Devil

Imagine a "spiritual bank account." We make daily withdrawals from it as we experience stress at work, watch television or movies, listen to certain kinds of music and even some conversations. Time spent with family and friends can sometimes drain us. A full day of living can sometimes exhaust us, and leave us spiritually spent.

If we make enough deposits throughout the day to balance the withdrawals, we end up with a spiritually balanced account. However, if we do not make the spiritual deposits to cover the spiritual demands, we end up spiritually short. We know those days because we do not feel balanced.

The spiritual deposit we make attending church on Sunday may not be enough to cover the spiritual withdrawals we make during the week. But for many of us, this is often the only spiritual deposit we make. We can avoid overdrafts and "bouncing spiritual checks" by consistently making spiritual deposits. Let us look at some ways we can do this.

Listen to the Prophets

The Doctrine and Covenants tells us if we will follow the words of our prophets and keep the commandments, "the gates of hell shall not prevail against you; yea, and the Lord God will disperse the powers of darkness from before you" (D&C 21:6).

A living prophet leads us today. The Savior Himself communicates with our prophet and reveals that which is for our good in our day and age. "And the voice of warning shall be unto all people, by the mouths of my disciples, whom I have chosen in these last days" (D&C 1:4; also see Amos 3:7). If we follow the prophet, Satan will not prevail against us.

A good gauge of how faithfully we follow our living prophet is in asking ourselves: "Do we see R-rated movies?" We all know the debates over watching R-rated movies. "It's not really that violent or that sexy," "Those scenes do not bother me," or "I can handle it." The mere fact that our prophet asks us to avoid these movies is reason enough not to see them. Where do we stand?

As we obey the prophet, we will be blessed and given added strength to overcome the tempter's power. We will see the Savior's way more clearly and grow in our desire to follow Him. "Whether by mine own voice or by the voice of my servants, it is the same" (D&C 1:38).

Daily Scripture Reading

Everywhere we turn, we are told to read the scriptures. There must be a reason. The Book of Mormon tells us, "Lay hold upon the word of God, which is quick and powerful, which shall divide asunder all the cunning and the snares and the wiles of the devil, and lead the man of Christ in a strait and narrow course across that everlasting gulf of misery which is prepared to engulf the wicked" (Helaman 3:29). The scriptures are a gift from God. They are "a lamp unto our feet" (Psalms 119:105) and will lead us through the "mist of darkness" and the "tempter's snares." Alternately, as we study the scriptures daily, search them, follow their counsel, and pray for answers to our questions, we will know the will of our Father in Heaven.

Daily Prayer

We are counseled to do "all things with prayer and thanksgiving" that we "may not be seduced by evil spirits, or doctrines of devils, or the commandments of men, for some are of men and others of devils" (D&C 46:7). Through prayer we develop a relationship with our Father in Heaven and learn to rely on Him daily. James tells us if we draw nigh unto God, He will draw nigh unto us (see James 4:7–8). Our hearts will fill with gratitude for all our blessings, and our eyes will see His hand upon our life. We will gain understanding and light that will help us discern right from wrong and overcome that which stands in our way.

Nephi tells us, "watch and pray always, lest ye be tempted by the devil, and ye be led away captive by him ... for Satan desireth to have you, that he may sift you as wheat. Therefore ye must always pray unto the Father in my name" (3 Nephi 18:15,18–19).

Fasting

Have you ever been away from the physical comforts of life or have met someone who lost everything they owned due to a flood, earthquakes, tornado, or other disaster? In these moments, what really matters? What desires rise to the surface? After we seek food, water, safety, and the basics of life, what becomes very clear is how grateful we are for family, friends, and life itself. Stripped from the material things of this world, we develop a greater awareness of our own spiritual self, our relationship with God, and what really matters. Some people experience a great sense of freedom, even happiness, when realizing we can feel peace and joy without any attachment to the things of this world.

Fasting helps us set aside the physical world and connects us to the things of the Spirit. We feel good after a day of fasting because we rise above the temporal matters of this world and develop greater sensitivity to the Holy Ghost. This sacrifice brings us spiritual blessings such as greater inner strength, greater awareness of Satan's snares, and a closer relationship with our Father in Heaven. We develop a spiritual base that provides clarity as to what really matters. From this base comes a sense of calm and true happiness. So instead of going through the loss of everything we have to reach this enlightenment, we are given the gift of fasting. Fasting is a sure way to find peace in an unstable world.

Living the Higher Law

The Savior introduced a way of living that went beyond self-indulgence, revenge, and seeking fairness—"an eye for an eye and a tooth for a tooth" as taught by the old Mosaic law (see Matthew 5:38). The Savior taught a higher law—"But I say unto you, Love your enemies, bless them that curse you, do good to them that hate you, and pray for them which despitefully use you, and persecute you" (Matthew 5:44).

The Savior went beyond "thou shall not kill" and admonished us not to even get mad—"whosoever is angry with his brother shall be in danger of His judgment" (Matthew 5:23–24). You see, if we work through the anger, we will likely never reach the point of an intentional killing.

The Savior also said, "Ye have heard that it was said by them of old time, Thou shalt not commit adultery: but I say unto you, That whosoever looketh on a woman to lust after her hath committed adultery with her already in his heart" (Matthew 5: 27–28). If we never look at another person with lust, we will never need to worry about committing adultery.

The Savior brought a higher law, not to make life more difficult but to give us more freedom. Living the higher law frees us from fear, addiction, misery, emptiness, and pain, and allows us the freedom of choice. We rise above and avoid those things that destroy. Living the Savior's way, however tough it may be at the moment, leads to joy and long-lasting happiness. In reality, living becomes freer and much easier.

Joining the Fold

Now if we think we can take on Satan and his armies as a single individual, forget it. The Savior knew the danger of the "one" lost from the fold and made a point of bringing him or her back into the safety of the fold. Friends, family, active attendance and fellowship in the Church provide support, strength, and encouragement. As we work together, we not only grow spiritually stronger ourselves, but our collective efforts become very powerful in building up righteousness and overcoming evil.

Humility

Sometimes we have to take off the armor of the natural man— all the defenses—be it selfishness, greed, or pride, and allow the Spirit of the Lord to penetrate our souls. Pride begins the process of hardening our hearts to the truth. "He that will harden his heart, the same receiveth the lesser portion of the word; and he that will not harden his heart, to him is given the greater portion of the word, until it is given unto him to know the mysteries of God until he know them in full" (Alma 12:10). Only when we are teachable, will the Spirit bear witness of truth and light to our spirits.

Hold Fast to Truth

Truth is truth no matter when, where, what, or why. "Truth is knowledge of things as they are, and as they were, and as they are to come" (D&C 93:24). "Truth abideth forever and ever" (D&C 1:39). We can reject, deny, and try to change truth, but no matter our reaction to it, truth will always remain the same.

God is the source of truth. "I am the light, and the life, and the truth of the world" (Ether 4:12). "Truth will I send forth out of the earth, to bear testimony of mine Only Begotten;...and truth will I cause to sweep the earth as with a flood, to gather out mine elect from the four quarters of the earth" (Moses 7:62). The Savior said, "I am the way, the truth, and the life" (John 14:6).

Brigham Young encouraged us to seek truth: "Whether a truth be found with professed infidels, or with the Universalists, or the Church of Rome, or the Methodists, the Church of

England, the Presbyterians, the Baptists, the Quakers, the Shakers, or any other of the various and numerous different sects and parties, all of whom have more or less truth, it is the business of the Elders of this Church (Jesus, their Elder Brother, being at their head) to gather up all the truths in the world pertaining to life and salvation, to the Gospel we preach,... to the sciences, and to philosophy, wherever it may be found in every nation, kindred, tongue, and people and bring it to Zion."[1] "Mormonism includes all truth."[2]

Truths exist in every area of life—at work, in our relationships, in learning, and within ourselves. When we do not align our lives with truth, we pay a price. On the other hand, when we seek the truth in all areas of life and hold fast to it, we can have an assurance that we are living in a manner pleasing to God. As a result, life becomes less complicated because living by truth provides clarity and stabilization in a world full of contradictions.

Reactions to Truth

Some people are not interested in truth. They love worldly things, pleasure, their passions, and themselves more than they love God. And because of their agency, they have a right to do so. Others seek truth, but when the pressures become too great and the darkness rises around them, they fold, not having the integrity or fortitude to hold fast to truth and endure the tough moments. Others fear man more than God and "[fall] away into forbidden paths and [are] lost" (1 Nephi 8:22–23).

Some seek truth by turning to the philosophies of men, losing their vision and understanding of God's ways. "When they are learned they think they are wise, and they hearken not unto the counsel of God, for they set it aside, supposing they know of themselves, wherefore, their wisdom is foolishness and it profiteth them not. And they shall perish" (2 Nephi 9:28).

Still others actually fight the good fight, hold to the rod, and make it through the dark periods of life (see 1 Nephi 8:24–28). They may even partake of the tree of life—God's love—and understand the goodness and mercy of God, but when the world "mocks" and makes fun of them, they are "ashamed," cannot hold up under the pressure, and fall.

Some of us think we are doing just fine and need nothing more. Thus, we stop progressing. Nephi, foretelling of our day and Satan's influence said, "Others will he pacify, and lull them away into carnal security, that they will say: All is well in Zion; yea Zion prospereth, all is well—and thus the devil cheateth their souls, and leadeth them away carefully down to hell" (2 Nephi 28:21). We have the truth—we see truth because the Spirit bears witness of it, but we go no further to make truth a part of our lives. We say, "All is well." "Wo be unto him that saith: We have received, and we need no more!" (2 Nephi 28:27; see also verses 29–30).

So where are we in relationship to truth? What level of desire, dedication, and commitment do we have to truth?

As we align our lives with truth, we find in ourselves a sense of confidence and peace, and we experience growth and goodness within. Simply put, truth fits. Going against truth negatively affects our efforts to feel confident "in the presence of God" (D&C 121:45). Moreover, we may even fight against light due to this discomfort.

Satan would have us rationalize, argue against, and overpower truth with self-interest. He would have us redefine it according to the popular ideas in our society. Satan would have us live outside the boundaries of truth. "And that wicked one cometh and taketh away light and truth, through disobedience, from the children of men" (D&C 93:39). However, truth will never change, whether we follow it or not.

Thank goodness, we have a way to know truth—asking in prayer and receiving personal revelation. As we remain loyal, that truth will turn to light and help us keep Satan at bay. The Savior said, "He that keepeth the commandments receiveth truth and light…light and truth forsake that evil one" (D&C 93:28).

Trusting God

Another way we can make deposits into our spiritual bank account is by trusting God daily. The Savior said, "Whosoever shall put their trust in God shall be supported in their trials, and in their troubles, and their afflictions, and shall be lifted up at the last day (Alma 36:3). Isaiah tells us that the Savior will give "power to the faint; and to them that have no might he increaseth strength…. But they that wait upon the Lord shall renew their strength; they shall mount up with wings as eagles; they shall run, and not be weary; and they shall walk, and not faint" (Isaiah 40:29–31).

And when we fall, "Rejoice not against me, O mine enemy: when I fall, I shall arise; when I sit in darkness, the Lord shall be a light unto me" (Micah 7:7–8).

When we truly wait upon the Lord, He delivers us by giving us renewed strength to run the race and not be weary, walk and not faint, no matter how rugged the path.

Nephi says, "O Lord, I have trusted in thee, and I will trust in thee forever. I will not put my trust in the arm of flesh; for I know that cursed is he that putteth his trust in the arm of flesh" (2 Nephi 4:34).

As we give up having to control and begin to trust in God, He will take the lead. The situation may not change, but we will feel His healing power as relief comes and the burden lifts.

Like the children of Israel who daily gathered manna for survival, we must gather our spiritual manna, feel God's love, and keep our spiritual bank accounts full each and every day. With God's help through the Holy Spirit we will conquer Satan's influences.

Notes

1. Brigham Young, *Discourses of Brigham Young*, 248.
2. Ibid., 3.

Chapter Twelve

BUILDING CHARACTER

KING ARTHUR LIVED IN A TIME when the sword was the rule. Violence, destruction, greed and power were the objectives. As king of Camelot, he dreamed of a better world where chivalry would replace savagery. He cautioned his people not to let passion destroy the dream. King Arthur created the Knights of the Round Table in the hope that the knights could help the people in his kingdom live his dream, that is, to live a better way.

King Arthur's integrity and commitment to his dream were tested when his wife, Guenevere, had an adulterous relationship with his dear friend and protégé, Lancelot. One of King Arthur's greatest challenges was dealing with this betrayal. If he gave in to revenge and did not follow the law, as he had required all others to do, he would go against all that he stood for—a "civilized king over a civilized society." His poor example would destroy any hope of a better world, of a people living by civil law, and, thus, would end the Knights of the Round Table.

Oh the struggle! As king, Arthur could have easily destroyed Lancelot and Guenevere by having their heads cut off. Those whom he loved most had given him the deepest betrayals. Oh the pain! As King Arthur loved his long-time friend and, even more deeply, his wife. His devotion and loyalty far exceeded common friendship and love, even with their betrayal. His commitment to live beyond the dictates of mere passion was just as deep. He argued, "Could it possibly be civilized to destroy the things I love? Could it possibly be civilized to love myself above all?"

King Arthur found resolve when he rose beyond passion and concluded: "We shall live through this together…they, and I. And may God have mercy on us all."[1]

One of the biggest betrayals in life is a break in trust, especially in a marriage vow. The agony any of us experiences from betrayal would be similar to King Arthur's struggle. He searched for the right thing to do as he toiled between the desires of a "man" and being true to the qualities of a "noble king." He demonstrated self-discipline and greatness, seeing beyond his own pain to live a higher law when he loved, forgave, and had compassion even for those whose passions created pain for him. He rose above the desires and passions that pull down and destroy and became a better person because of it. What a struggle, but, in the end, what victory! He possessed true nobility!

Cinderella faced severe challenges! Both of her parents died in her early years, and she was left to be abused and neglected by a self-centered stepmother and stepsisters. Most would be bitter and ugly on the inside with the constant abuse from the outside world. However, Cinderella was neither bitter nor ugly. How did this happen? How did she become so beautiful and her stepsisters so ugly?

Could it be that her beauty developed because she rose above her circumstances allowing her sense of integrity to help her be true to what she knew she needed to be, no matter the situation? Perhaps Cinderella was not beautiful by nature. She certainly was not by the looks of her everyday clothes or the way she wore her hair. She wore rags, and her hands must have been rough from all the work, cleaning, and abuse she tolerated.

There must have been other women at the ball dressed as beautifully as she. But in this story, no one compared to Cinderella's beauty, not even those with wealth or prestige. Cinderella was poor with no name or honor, yet she stood out. Perhaps rare beauty, created by true character caused her to shine above all present.

Maybe through it all, her hope and trust in a higher power helped her to keep perspective and connected to that which is beautiful in the world. Although taken to her limits, perhaps the power of her faith created the miracle, and, as a result, the finishing touches to her beauty.

Cinderella's ugly stepsisters, on the other hand, might have become ugly because of their self-indulgence, bitterness, jealousy, and self-centeredness. The more they indulged themselves and remained self-centered, the more unattractive they became. Perhaps had Cinderella lowered herself to the level of her stepsisters, she would have become as repulsive and unpleasant. Had they risen above their selfishness, they might have developed the qualities and beauty of Cinderella!

Some psychology books today talk about the "Cinderella Syndrome" and identify Cinderella as a young woman simply waiting for a prince to rescue her from her circumstances. Perhaps a deeper, more accurate version would illustrate how Cinderella remained true to what she knew mattered—kindness and integrity. She did not stoop to belittling or betraying others which is perhaps what made her more beautiful and even noble. And, as water rises to meet its own level, nobility attracts nobility.

In his book *As a Man Thinketh*, James Allen writes, "He who lives constantly in the conception of noble and lofty thoughts, who dwells upon all that is pure and unselfish, will as surely as the sun reaches its zenith and the moon its full, become wise and noble in character, and rise into a position of influence, and blessedness."[2]

He goes on to say, "A noble and Godlike character is not a thing of favor or chance, but is the natural result of continued effort in right thinking, the effect of long-cherished association with Godlike thoughts."[3]

Few individuals in this life reach a well balanced, finished, noble character. But these are the very people whose calm, serene demeanor we seek and revere. We bask in their presence like fresh water when thirsty or a cool breeze when hot and exhausted. These noble people rise to the occasion no matter how exacting or unfair, no matter the conditions, always remaining calm, true, and poised.

Many of us forget that we are all noble by nature! We are all princes and princesses in the making, to become kings and queens in God's royal kingdom on high. Although Cinderella was a fictional character, would that same level of integrity, if not a greater level, be expected of us in order to qualify for such a royal position and place of honor in the kingdom of God? Will we not need to develop the nobility and character of a king or queen, a god? And how *will* we, unless we are taken to our limits and have the opportunity to make the choices that develop character and, thus, nobility?

Sometimes we forget, ignore, or do not recognize our inner nobility. Certainly, the self indulging and self-centered part of the world around us encourages us to live on a lesser, even mediocre level. As we listen and conform our lives to these ways, we often become much less than our true selves. Hence, we do not reach the level of character that matches our divine heritage.

When we are true to our inner nobility and live by what we know is right, we rise above our shortcomings. We become anchored in virtue, never attacking or criticizing, but gracious and kind. We develop an inner peace, even through the storms. That peace shines in our countenance and will attract others.

Now you may say, "It's easy to make up stories of individuals who have risen above the natural man and remained true to what they know is right in the midst of sorrow and challenges, and still have grown and changed. But, can this really happen? What about real life?"

One of the great men in history, Benjamin Franklin, demonstrated this great principle. The story goes that as a young boy, Ben was rambunctious, annoying, hyperactive, and probably would have been diagnosed today with Attention Deficit and Hyperactivity Disorder. In his early teens, an older gentleman told young Ben if he did not change his ways, he would grow up to have no friends and end up a very lonely person. Ben was affected by what was said and spent a good deal of time pondering what he could do to alter such a fate.

Determined to have friends, Ben made a list of thirteen qualities he knew would help him make and keep friends. Each week for the next thirteen weeks, young Ben focused on incorporating one quality a week into his life and personality. When the thirteen weeks were finished, he started the same process all over again. Benjamin Franklin continued this pattern throughout his life.

Years later, well into his eighties, when the Founding Fathers were struggling to write the Constitution of the United States, Benjamin Franklin found himself a part of that great historic event. The conflicts were huge as many strong personalities were involved. Without some intervention, the Constitution as we know it might never have existed.

Ben Franklin—the same young man despised as a child and warned that he would never have friends if he did not change his ways—was the very person who monitored and tempered the disputes. Because of his presence, the Constitution was completed, and from that point on, Benjamin Franklin became known as the "peacemaker of the Constitution."

Ben Franklin's life-long dedication and sacrifice allowed him to intervene when no one else could. Consequently, he is one of the most revered men in United States history.

Joseph of old is another example of character building. He moved beyond the natural self, even through adversity. He was rejected, deceived, and sold as a slave by his own brothers to a caravan of Midianites. They in turn sold him as a slave to the house of Potiphar, one of the men chief under the great Pharaoh of Egypt. Joseph spent years as a slave under likely near unbearable conditions.

One day, Potiphar's wife falsely accused Joseph of making advances toward her. As a person of integrity and good character, young Joseph actually ran from her immoral advances. He was thrown into prison for her lies but never wavered. Even in the lowest of circumstances, he became a leader among prisoners. When presented before the Pharaoh to interpret a dream, the Pharaoh himself recognized Joseph's uniqueness. In time, the Pharaoh made Joseph second in command over all of Egypt.

Years later, Joseph's brothers searched for food in Egypt because of a severe, seven-year drought. Not knowing whom they approached, they plead for help. Joseph could have denied their plea, justifying it as payback for their disloyalty years earlier. He could have had them all imprisoned or hung. Instead, he rose above his anger and resentment, above the pain and suffering, and helped the very ones who had abused and betrayed him. That is true nobility!

President David O. McKay said, "Man's chief concern in life should not be the acquiring of gold, or of fame, or of material possessions. It should not be the development of physical prowess, nor of intellectual strength, but his aim, the highest in life, should be the development of Christlike character." He goes on to say, "He [the Savior] is our pattern."[4]

Developing Character

So how do we develop the character to build true nobility as our Heavenly Father desires? How do we stay committed to the process? First, we must recognize we all have the potential to become more than we are. We also must recognize that it is critical that we make changes. The whole concept behind repentance is that we improve and become more like Christ.

Nobility requires being true to our divine heritage, regardless of the circumstances or situation. This means holding fast to truth and trusting God even when it does not make sense to us, no matter the adversity or the pressures of the moment.

Becoming More than Who We Are

Hugh B. Brown shared an example of building character the Lord's way. He starts by telling his famous story of the currant bush. In his own words, President Brown shares the following:

> I went out one morning and saw a currant bush. It had grown up over six feet high. It was going all to wood. There were no blossoms and no currants.... So I got some pruning shears and went after it. I cut it down, and pruned it, until there was nothing left but a little clump of stems.

It was just coming daylight, and I thought I saw on top of each of these little stumps what appeared to be a tear, and I thought the currant bush was crying. I thought I heard that currant bush talk. And I thought I heard it say: "How could you do this to me? I was making such wonderful growth. I was almost as big as the shade tree and the fruit tree that are inside the fence, and now you have cut me down. Every plant in the garden will look down on me, because I didn't make what I should have made. How could you do this to me? I thought you were the gardener here."

I thought it so much that I answered. I said, "Look, little currant bush, I am the gardener here, and I know what I want you to be.... If I had allowed you to continue to grow as you had started, all your strength would have gone to wood; your roots would not have gained a firm hold, and the purpose for which I brought you into my garden would have been defeated. Your place would have been taken by another, for you would have been barren. You must not weep. All this will be for your good, and some day, when you see more clearly, when you are richly laden with luscious fruit, you will thank me and say, 'Surely, he knew the purpose of my being, and I thank him now for what I then thought was cruelty.'"[5]

Hugh B. Brown went on to tell of his experience in the Royal Army. He made rapid progress through the ranks and was proud of his position as a field officer in the British Canadian Army. Then came the day when Officer Brown was next in line for the office of general in the British Army—something he had wanted for years. His pride swelled as he was called in for the interview.

As soon as Officer Brown sat down the interviewing general told him, "I'm sorry I cannot make the appointment. You are entitled to it. You have passed all the examinations. You have the seniority. You've been a good officer, but I can't make the appointment.

You are to return to Canada and become a training officer and a transport officer. Someone else will be made a general."

When the general left the room to answer a phone call, Hugh B. Brown saw his personal history sheet on the desk. Across the bottom was written, in bold, "**THIS MAN IS A MORMON.**" He goes on to say that in those days Mormons were not very well liked.

President Brown returned on the train to his hometown broken hearted and with bitterness in his soul. He said, "Every click of the wheels on the rails seemed to say, 'You are a failure. You will be called a coward when you get home.' I was so bitter that I threw my cap and my saddle brown belt on the cot, I clenched my fists and I shook them at heaven. I said, 'How could you do this to me, God? I have done everything I could do to measure up. There is nothing that I could have done—that I should have done—that I haven't done. How could you do this to me?' I was as bitter as gall.

"And then I heard a voice, and I recognized the tone of this voice. It was my own voice, and the voice said, 'I am the gardener here. I know what I want you to do.'" He continued, "The bitterness went out of my soul, and I fell on my knees by the cot to ask forgiveness for my ungratefulness and my bitterness."

In the next room, a group of Latter-day Saint service men were meeting for their Tuesday MIA meeting. He said, "As I was kneeling there, praying for forgiveness, I heard their voices singing:

It may not be on the mountain height
Or over the stormy sea,
It may not be at the battle's front
My Lord will have need of me.
But if, by a still, small voice he calls

To paths that I do not know,
I'll answer, dear Lord, with my hand in thine:
I'll go where you want me to go.[6]

President Brown rose from his knees, a more humble man. Fifty years later, an Apostle of the Lord, he said "I look up to him and say, 'Thank you, Mr. Gardener, for cutting me down, for loving me enough to hurt me.' I see now that it was wise that I should not become a general at that time, because if I had I would have been senior officer of all western Canada, with a lifelong, handsome salary, a place to live, and a pension when I'm no good any longer, but I would have raised my six daughters and two sons in army barracks. They would no doubt have married out of the Church, and I think I would not have amounted to anything…. I have done better than I would have done if the Lord had let me go the way I wanted to go."[7]

Often, when faced with an unexpected ordeal, we can easily become angry and bitter. But, like President Brown, if we put our trust in the master Gardener, we will grow and develop qualities of true nobility.

Sometimes as single individuals on our own, it is hard to hold fast to the iron rod, especially when no one is looking. As they say, "It is how we are when no one else is around that measures our true character." Going through life solo is yet another opportunity to build character. Maybe this is part of the reason we are yet single. If we make correct choices when no one is watching, trust God despite the pressure to do otherwise, and not be afraid of improvement, we have a wonderful opportunity for growth and character building.

A Mustard Seed

Do not think we develop nobility overnight or have to be a big shot to prove our worthiness. Our Father in Heaven often works through small and simple means to make great things—as with a mustard seed, "which indeed is the least of all seeds; but when it is grown, it is the greatest among herbs, and becometh a tree, so that the birds of the air come and lodge in the branches thereof" (Matthew 13: 32). It is small in form, powerful in influence. Oh, that we would follow the example of a mustard seed as we strive to build our character and nobility from the small and simple within us—small in form, powerful in influence!

THE REFINER'S FIRE

At one time or another our path in life will lead us into the refiner's fire. "For he is like a refiner's fire, . . . And he shall sit as a refiner and purifier" (3 Nephi 24:2–3). As the verse implies, there is a refining process that burns out the old and creates the new. If we desire the kind of character that fits our true heritage—being a son or daughter of the Eternal God—and expect to live with such royalty and feel comfortable, we then must expect to be refined, purified, and have our character shaped into nobility.

Think of Abraham, Isaac, Moses, and of the pioneers who struggled with character, faith, and courage through severe adversities. Can we see ourselves standing next to such great individuals in that day when our Heavenly Father gathers us all around Him? Will we feel equal in caliber with these faithful leaders and followers who remained true and followed the Savior no matter the circumstances? Will we feel comfortable?

Elder M. Russell Ballard said, "Although our journeys today are less demanding physically than the trek of our pioneers 150 years ago, they are no less challenging. . . . It will require every bit of our strength, wisdom, and energy to overcome the obstacles that will confront us. But even that will not be enough. We will learn, as did our pioneer ancestors, that it is only in faith—*real* faith, whole-souled, tested and tried—that we will find safety and confidence as we walk our own perilous pathways through life."⁸

A diamond in the rough does not look like a jewel. But once refined, it becomes a beautiful and precious gem for all to see and value. So we, to become kings and queens, must expect a refining, fiery, finishing process. It is one of the reasons we are here on earth—to build the character and nobility which will prepare us to meet God (see Alma 12:24).

You could say, "That's fine, as long as it does not get in the way of my Sunday game on television or require me to change or to give up any of my bad habits." However, because it is the refining process, it will zero in on the very passions, fears, and desires that connect us to anything other than God and godliness. The refiner's fire will take us to our core values, even to the event that will drop us to our knees.

Of course, no one forces us to engage in this process. The choice is completely up to us, but maybe the following analogy will help make sense of this refining process.

The Invisible Hourglass

Imagine, each one of us in our own spiritual, bigger than life, invisible hourglass. This hourglass has a very wide bottom representing self-centered living, a narrow center representing the refining process, and a wide open top representing Christ-centered living. Imagine that we all start at the bottom, on the floor of our own spiritual hour glass. We can choose to stay there as it takes no effort to sit at the bottom. Initially there is a lot of room and we feel good. We have no real responsibility and it feels like freedom. Let's say here we can give into every wish, passion, and desire, and be as self-indulgent as we want to be. We have that choice.

But notice what happens. One by one, each grain of sand—be they moments of sin, passion, selfish desire, pride, impatience, apathy, greed, or fear—tumbles down through the narrow neck of our hour glass to build what in the end is a huge pile of debris. If we do not make the effort to rise above this falling rubble, one by one, we slowly but surely begin to be buried by it.

All this self-gratification, although initially pleasurable, can trap us in the end. It can become our greatest source of misery as we desperately fight for true freedom from the bondage created by our sin and self-indulgence.

In fact, at this level, we only experience ourselves as our actions are inward and selfish. With this shortsightedness, we often connect to illusions of self-importance and aggrandizement. Those who make no effort to rise above this weighty pile cheat themselves of the fullness of life. They can feel empty and wonder why they are so unhappy.

Neal A. Maxwell commented, "Unchecked selfishness...stubbornly blocks the way for developing all of the divine qualities: love, mercy, patience, long-suffering, kindness, graciousness, goodness, and gentleness.... The man and woman of Christ are easily entreated, but the selfish person is not. Christ never brushed aside those in need because He had bigger things to do! Furthermore, the men and women of Christ are constant, being the same in private as in public. We cannot keep two sets of books while heaven has but one."[9]

One of the dilemmas of being single is our tendency to be self-focused, as everything we do is usually for ourselves such as cleaning the house, food shopping, and earning a paycheck. Our challenge is to make the effort to move beyond our own selves and passions.

The Straight and Narrow

Imagine the narrow neck of our invisible, spiritual hourglass as the refining process. We are not only asked to rise above the fallen debris of sin, but now we are expected to work our way through this "straight and narrow" passage (Matthew 7:14).

Being in the refining process, we can expect to experience growing pains, as refinement usually involves a moment of truth, even the trial of our lives. These critical moments may involve hurt, fear, rejection, stress, isolation, or even the lack of our emotional needs being met.

The choices we make to move through the refining process or move away from it determine our movement toward Christ-centered living, the top half of our hourglass, or self-centered living, the bottom of the hourglass.

Our "natural" selves would want to avoid this refining process. Outside forces may attempt to convince us that this process is too painful and not necessary. The reality is that the pain we experience in our efforts to grow toward Christ-centered living is not as great as the misery of one who is trapped under his own experiences of the passion and sin of self-centered living.

In fact, the growing pains we experience occur as we give up the lesser self and shed the defenses and fear used to avoid God and His Spirit. When we grow spiritually, we not only develop more strength to continue moving toward Christ centered living but we also develop greater depth and understanding of the purpose of life. We begin experiencing the source of peace, joy, wisdom, grace, truth, charity, and love.

Christ-Centered Living

As we grow, we develop greater sensitivity toward others as well as toward everything around us—the beauty of nature, the needs of a child, of parents, and of friends. We develop a greater understanding of our own needs and better ways to meet them. We enjoy a sense of freedom as we move beyond ourselves, finding balance and joy as we serve and love. Relying on and having faith in God, we find that we develop attributes of our Heavenly Father.

Eternal Life

Christ-Centered Living

Knowing Christ

Meeting measure of our creation

True freedom

Peace, wisdom, joy, happiness

Awareness of Savior's influence in our life

Awareness of others and their needs

Better understanding of gospel principles

Trying to keep commandments

Following the Spirit

Letting go of sin

Faith in Christ

*Our choice to
move up or down*   MOMENT OF TRUTH   *Straight and
narrow way*

Trial of our life

Self-indulgence

Illusion of freedom

Illusion of self-importance

Some guilt

Anger or depression

Loss of guilt and gospel understanding

Overwhelmed/weathered

Desperate for freedom

Misery/pain/emptiness

Self-Centered Living

Self-Destruction

We cannot expect to reach a level of nobility over night. The scriptures tell us all things are to be "done in wisdom and order, for it is not requisite that a man should run faster than he has strength. And again, it is expedient that he should be diligent, that thereby he might win the prize; therefore, all things must be done in order" (Mosiah 4:47). We are admonished to run the race with patience.

The gospel also tells us that the process requires total commitment. We are to "follow the Son, with full purpose of heart, acting no hypocrisy and no deception before God, but with real intent" (2 Nephi 31:13). In other words, we cannot fake this process but must be one in mind, heart, and action with Christ.

The most important point is that the only way we can make it through the weight and pressure of the refining process is by placing the Savior at the center of our lives with complete and total reliance and trust. By submitting to our Father in Heaven's will, following the Spirit, and relying on Jesus Christ, we develop the strength to endure and succeed. "Then shall thy confidence wax strong in the presence of God" (D&C 121:45–46). Our burden lightens because the Savior now walks with us and helps us carry our load (see Matthew 11:28–30).

Now those buried under the self-indulgence of pride, sin, and passion can still make it out from under the debris but it requires what is required of all of us—to bring Christ's atoning sacrifice to bear in our lives. Only the Savior can wash away the dirt and provide freedom for those once buried under such a load. Once released from the misery of sin, we begin the same trek that all must take to ultimately return to our Heavenly Father's presence.

President Spencer W. Kimball said, "No pain that we suffer, no trial that we experience is wasted .... All that we endure, especially when we endure it patiently, builds up our characters, our hearts, expands our souls, and makes us more tender and charitable.... It is through sorrow, suffering, toil, and tribulation, that we gain the education that we come here to acquire and which will make us more like our Father and Mother in heaven."[10]

It is our choice to discipline the mind and feed the soul. Joseph Smith said, "I teach them correct principles, and they govern themselves."[11] As we remain on the path, even during the refining process of life, we will reach nobility and a Christlike character. And what is the ultimate benefit? We will have God's Spirit and presence in our lives, bringing with it a sense of joy and happiness and eternal life in His presence in the hereafter.

The Ultimate Test

Corrie Ten Boom shares in her book *The Hiding Place* an experience that required her to use character and integrity to move beyond her natural self. Only through the Savior's help could she reach this level. A prisoner at a war camp in Germany during WWII, she wrote:

> It was at a church service in Munich that I saw him, the former S.S. man who had stood guard at the shower room door in the processing center at Ravensbruck. He was the first of our actual jailers that I had seen since that time. And suddenly it was all there—the roomfull of mocking men, the heaps of clothing, Betsie's pain-blanched face.
>
> He came up to me as the church was emptying, beaming and bowing. "How grateful I am for your message, *Fraulein*," he said. "To think that, as you say, He has washed my sins away!"
>
> His hand was thrust out to shake mine. And I, who had preached so often to the people in Bloemendaal the need to forgive, kept my hand at my side.
>
> Even as the angry, vengeful thoughts boiled through me, I saw the sin of them. Jesus Christ had died for this man; was I

going to ask for more? Lord Jesus, I prayed, forgive me and help me to forgive him.

I tried to smile, I struggled to raise my hand. I could not. I felt nothing, not the slightest spark of warmth or charity. And so again I breathed a silent prayer. Jesus, I cannot forgive him. Give me Your forgiveness.

As I took his hand the most incredible thing happened. From my shoulder along my arm and through my hand a current seemed to pass from me to him, while into my heart sprang a love for this stranger that almost overwhelmed me.

And so I discovered that it is not on our forgiveness any more than on our goodness that the world's healing hinges, but on His. When He tells us to love our enemies, He gives, along with the command, the love itself.[12]

Joseph Smith demonstrated tremendous character when Ezra Booth, a former member of the Church, wrote letters about the Prophet to the local newspapers spreading lies and rumors. A group of drunken men, believing the letters to be truthful, attacked Joseph Smith when he was up late caring for an adopted son who was sick with measles. The mob entered the Prophet's home, choked him, ripped off his clothes, and attempted to pour acid and hot tar down his throat. During the ordeal, the bottle of acid broke off a portion of Joseph's tooth, which caused a whistle in his speech for the rest of his life. Severely cut, hot tar spread over his body, and covered with feathers, Joseph was left for dead.

Signey Rigdon was also beaten, knocked unconscious, and was delirious for days. Sadly, the baby Joseph was caring for died from cold exposure of that night.

Joseph's friends helped clean off the tar, a very painful and lengthy process that took hours. Still, the next day Joseph went to church and preached as usual. Some in the congregation were members of the mob who had tarred and feathered Joseph. Even with the pain of his wounds, Joseph delivered his sermon without mentioning the violence of the night before, unwavering in his commitment to God. That afternoon, he baptized three individuals.

The ultimate example of character belongs to our Savior. What would have happened to the whole plan of salvation if the Savior had succumbed to temporal desires and sought revenge? During the events surrounding His Crucifixion, He could have made the skies fall on those who hurt Him. The Savior could have struck down every person around Him when they were mocking Him, and falsely accusing Him. He could have allowed the natural self, which He also possessed, to take over.

But Jesus did not. Why? For one thing, He was going about his Father's business. Secondly, He possessed complete and unconditional love in His heart, and desired that all, even the very people who tortured Him, might have eternal life. He knew that the soldiers at the cross had no idea what they were doing, or to whom they were doing it. The Savior had learned throughout his mortal existence line upon line, precept upon precept, even through suffering, and had reached a level of unconditional love. He let go of His own desires and the natural self to give us an example of loving, regardless of the circumstances.

The Savior gave the ultimate example of true nobility for the entire world and the greatest message of all time. Everything in the Savior's life was manifested in this one great moment of forgiveness at the cross. Not only was the great Atonement taking place, but when He said, "Father forgive them for they know not what they do," I believe the Savior was basically saying, "I love them, in spite of..., besides the fact..., no matter what." He showed us the ultimate example of nobility and true character at its finest. The Savior loved anyway!

Just like Jesus, we are to grow line upon line and precept upon precept, and become better for having these earthly experiences, no matter how painful. This means we will experience, at some level, what Jesus experienced so we can develop the character and nobility that helps us rise above our self-centered desires and love no matter what. It means we will plead, "Let me see it how you see it. Let me feel it how you would feel it. Let me love how you, God, would love. Let 'Thy will be done.'" Thus, we will have built a Christlike character fitting of our divine heritage and will be ready for our Father in Heaven's royal Kingdom on high.

Notes

1. Alan Jay Lerner, *Camelot.*

2. James Allen, *As a Man Thinketh,* 49.

3. Ibid., 2.

4. David O. McKay, *Pathway to Happiness,* comp. Llewelyn R. McKay (1961), 19.

5. Hugh B. Brown, *Relief Society Magazine,* June 1958, 354.

6. "It May Not Be on the Mountain Height," *Hymns of The Church of Jesus Christ of Latter-day Saints,* (1948), no. 75.

7. Hugh B. Brown, "The Currant Bush," *New Era,* January 1973, 14.

8. M. Russell Ballard, "You Have Nothing to Fear from the Journey," *Ensign,* May 1997, 59–61.

9. Neal A. Maxwell, "Put Off the Natural Man, and Come Off Conqueror," *Ensign,* November 1990, 14.

10. Spencer W. Kimball, *Tragedy or Destiny,* 4.

11. Joseph Smith, quoted in John Taylor, "The Organization of the Church," *Millennial Star,* November 15, 1851, 339.

12. Corrie Ten Boom with John and Elizabeth Sherrill, *The Hiding Place,* (1971), 238.

Part Four
BEING SINGLE

Chapter Thirteen

CREATING GREAT COMPANIONSHIPS

PRESIDENT GORDON B. HINCKLEY authored a pamphlet, *The Wonderful Thing That Is You and the Wonderful Good You Can Do,* in which he titled a section "Cultivate Great Companionships." Inspired by his thoughts, this chapter is dedicated to companionships.

What kinds of relationships and with whom and what determine great companionships? How are they cultivated? Let's look at some interactions with others and from there explore many other resources that offer us companionship.

Others

Good friends

President Hinckley stated, "Cultivate the companionships of good friends in whose lives you can find qualities worth bringing into your own lives."[1] In other words, choose carefully our associates and then look for qualities in them that would positively affect our lives. President Hinckley told of a time when he interviewed some missionaries and asked what quality they saw in their companions that they would like to incorporate into their own lives. He said many just stared at him; they had obviously never looked at their companions in such a way. Incorporating President Hinckley's question into our lives, we can ask ourselves what qualities of our friends would we like to incorporate into our lives?

Some might think it un-Christlike to be particular with whom we associate. The Savior said, "Fear not they which kill the body, but are not able to kill the soul, but rather fear him which is able to destroy both soul and body in hell" (Matthew 10:28). He continues, "Be ye therefore wise as serpents; and harmless as doves" (Matthew 10:16).

An Indian fable tells of the rattlesnake that asked a young boy to carry him across the river. The young boy answered, "You are a rattlesnake and will bite me." The snake assured the boy he would not bite him, and so the boy took the snake across the river. Once across the river, the rattlesnake bit the boy. When the boy countered "You promised not to bite me," the snake said, "You knew I was a rattlesnake when you took me across the river. Why would you expect anything different?"

Jesus said to love everyone, but that does not mean spending time with those whose influence could have devastating effects on us. We must love ourselves enough to want friends who are of good character. If we allow their positive traits to influence us and we share what we have learned with others, we end up with opportunities for the growth and development of wonderful relationships. We all benefit from such relationships and are blessed for having known one another.

(For a discussion on healthy dating relationships and positive potential partners, refer to the appendix.)

Family

Children—nephews, nieces, younger siblings, or our own—are a great source of happiness. But, like anything else, it takes time to cultivate those companionships. They need nurturing, attention, and love in order for their character and personality to take root and grow. Being a part of this process not only brings joy to the ones we serve but provides enjoyment in our own lives as well.

If we are childless, we can offer what parents often cannot—time, one-on-one experiences, mentoring, guidance, and support. We can introduce them to wonderful new worlds and, in return, we discover new worlds through their youthful eyes.

Sometimes we do not realize children endure the same losses as adults. After all, divorce or death of a loved one does not happen to parents only. They, too, need support during their grieving, perhaps even more than adults, as their understanding is limited and the likelihood of them blaming themselves is high. Because so many of us are caught in our own issues and feelings, we often do not pay attention to our children's pain nor do we provide the support they need. As we support them and fill their need to be loved and valued, they will have more energy to give back.

Siblings are another great source of companionship. Who else knows us and has a common life history more than our brothers and sisters? For this very reason, they may be the only ones who understand.

Sometimes these relationships need mending. We can initiate kindness and support these relationships, even if they do not return what we offer them. As we do, we will find peace because we are doing what the Savior would have us do—to love and to serve anyway.

We can be kind to our parents and work to get over any anger or resentment we might have toward them knowing they did the best they could with what they knew when parenting us. We knew before we came to earth what our situation in life would be. We eagerly agreed to come here, probably saying something to God like, "I'll show you I can handle this, no matter the circumstances or conditions! I'll make it back to you; you just watch and see!"

The interesting part about Heavenly Father's plan is that God gave the responsibility of raising children to human beings—ordinary men and women with imperfect traits. Thus, somewhere, somehow, sometime, those imperfections affect the children we raise—as if part of the plan guarantees imperfection. We then spend our lives overcoming those imperfections.

Perhaps up to age eighteen, we can blame our parents for our problems, but once we are adults, we are responsible to take care of ourselves, heal childhood wounds, stop blaming, and grow beyond the issues.

Just like everything else, we will not find perfection on our own. This is where the plan is twofold. These childhood issues not only humble us by giving us something to work on, but through the growing process, we learn to rely upon God—for we only reach perfect wholeness through Him. We can be bitter or we can be better. We choose, we decide. Moreover, by growing beyond these issues and cultivating our relationships with our parents we can develop with them a great source of joy. We can even experience a sense of gratitude for the good they provided.

Service as a Companion

We cannot cultivate relationships without service. So, too, service is a great companion in and of itself. Filling our lives with service helps us reach outside ourselves as we set aside our personal interest for a while and focus on someone else's needs. In doing so, we may also find new and great relationships. Our self-esteem, our sensitivity toward others and our capacity to love grow. In addition, our understanding of what really matters in life unfolds.

President Monson said, "That which you selfishly keep, you lose; that which you willingly share, you keep."[2] "He that findeth his life shall lose it: and he that loseth his life for my sake shall find it" (Matthew 10:39). The happiest people in the Church, married or single, are those who find ways to reach outside themselves and serve. Service is a great blessing when we feel down, alone, or helpless.

President Hinckley encouraged singles to reach out to those "whose problems are more serious than are yours. There are many boys and girls who fail in school for want of a little personal attention and encouragement. There are many elderly people who live in misery and loneliness and fear for whom a single conversation would bring a measure of hope and brightness."[3]

The Savior taught, "Whosoever will be chief among you, let him be your servant" (Matthew 20:27). He who was the greatest among us demonstrated this teaching as He dedicated His life to serving us all.

Placing Christ at the center of our service, as if He were doing it, we get lost in the task part of the service and begin to love in the way the Savior would love. As those we serve respond to our help, they experience God through us and, hence, come closer to God.

Christ-centered service also opens up the windows of heaven through which great blessings pour. Our vision clears, our burdens lighten, and our understanding of our mission here on Earth widens. We find forgiveness for our sins and spiritual healing. As we seek to bless, we will be blessed.

Cultivate a Great Companionship with Yourself

When we love ourselves, we take care of ourselves. We watch what we put into our bodies, into our minds, and into our hearts and souls. By surrounding ourselves with, for instance, good friends, good music, good entertainment, we find those things that inspire, uplift, and help us grow. When we truly care about ourselves, we develop self-discipline, letting go of what we want at the moment for what is best for us in the long run. We become our own best friend.

As we take time to know ourselves, we will realize just how unique and wonderful we truly are. We will realize that no other human being has ever been or ever will be just like we are—our talents, looks, mind, and feelings are unique. Not only does no one think, feel, and see the world exactly the same, but no one can offer what we each can offer! With humility and confidence, we can begin sharing what only we can share with the world around us. We become the greatest gift only we can offer.

Our happiness and fulfillment in life are rooted in our capacity to truly comprehend our divine nature and feel our Father in Heaven's love. Once we understand we are sons and daughters of a God who loves us, we never lack in self-regard, and we carry a sense of peace and confidence needed to accomplish that which God has in store for us. We no longer wait for the ideal time to share ourselves, our time, talents, and love, and we begin fitting the blueprint specifically designed for us, giving to the world what God intended for us to give.

What better time in life is there to focus on self-improvement than during our single years? A member of a stake Relief Society presidency, when engaged in a discussion with some singles, expressed her envy for the time the unmarried members had to focus on self-improvement. She commented on how it seemed to her that most singles tend to have a closer relationship with their Father in Heaven than the general population of the Church. When no one else is around, He is. As we build a relationship with our Father in Heaven and with ourselves, we will discover just how much we can offer others.

When asked, "What can be worse than being blind?" Helen Keller replied, "Having eyes to see but no vision." As we develop our talents and gifts, we discover God's love in our lives; we gain a sense of who we are and of God's plan for us. We begin reaching the full measure of our creation as our Father in Heaven intended.

Our Sacred Grove

A Sunday School teacher challenged his young adult class to find their own "sacred grove." He explained how all the great leaders of the past had their quiet and sacred places where they could find refuge, meditate, and seek divine guidance. Christ found refuge when He went into the desert (see Matthew 4:1–11). Moses climbed the mountain and received manifestations from God. Enos communicated with God through prayer in the forest and received a remission of his sins. Early one morning, with everything fresh and no one to disturb him, Joseph Smith entered the woods where he communicated with God, a place that became sacred to him (see Joseph Smith—History 1:14–17).

We each need time and a place where we can be alone, meditate and pray, and reconnect with God, the Spirit, and our own inner self that often gets lost in this hectic day and age. This place needs to be where we can find peace and quiet, away from loud and chaotic noises so we can feel the Spirit. For many, nature rejuvenates and inspires. For others, a quiet room can be a refuge and place of peace.

By sitting quietly, letting the noise of our minds pass, pouring out our hearts to God and then listening, we begin to discern the will of the Father and get to know our inner selves. The quiet and peace the Spirit brings can rejuvenate our souls. We can develop a depth of appreciation not only for the immediate surroundings and the beauty and refreshment of our environment, but also for the simple things in life, and the peace, insight, and assurance of God's inspiring influence. We will learn of God's interest in us and understand and bask in His love. We develop a sense of joy as we realize He is there for us if we but provide the space, peace, and quiet, and then listen.

The Temple

How many times are our lives halted and we find ourselves in circumstances we never expected, feeling confused and overwhelmed? How often do we need help keeping perspective and priorities right? How often do we need an answer to prayer?

Boyd K. Packer, in his booklet, *The Holy Temple,* wrote, "When members of the Church are troubled or when crucial decisions weigh heavily upon their minds, it is a common thing for them to go to the temple. It is a good place to take our cares. In the temple we can receive spiritual perspective. There, during the time of the temple service, we are 'out of the world.'"[4]

The temple teaches us on two levels. First, the temple endowment teaches us the meaning *of* life. Second, we gain a perspective *on* life through prayer, fasting, and pondering as we take questions to the temple and receive inspiration. Boyd K. Packer stated, "Sometimes our minds are so beset with problems, and there are so many things clamoring for attention at once, that we just cannot think clearly and see clearly. At the temple the dust of distraction seems to settle out, the fog and the haze seem to lift, and we can 'see' things that we were not able to see before and find a way through our troubles that we had not previously known."[5]

As we fast, ponder, and attend the temple with the proper attitude, we will receive the needed inspiration. If we do not have a clear understanding or answer by the time the endowment session ends, we can quietly sit in the celestial room pondering, praying, and listening to the Spirit until the answer comes.

The mere atmosphere of the temple softens our exterior shells of pride, selfishness, worldliness, and anger. It provides peace, fills our hearts with love, and rejuvenates our souls. President Hinckley said, "If we are a temple-going people, we will be a better people."[6]

There is a deep awakening or "change of heart" for those who have "ears to hear and eyes to see." It requires the sacrifice of our pride, sins, and apathy in order to open the lines of communion with God, even in the temple. When we humble ourselves and commune with God, we discover He is right there beside us. We gain an eternal perspective that lets us know what really matters. These experiences heal our wounds and fill our souls.

In a world where evil is everywhere and Satan has great power, it is wonderful to know that the house of the Lord is here for us.

Books

The Lord said, "Seek ye out of the best books words of wisdom; seek learning, even by study and also by faith" (D&C 88:118). President Hinckley counseled, "Cultivate the companionship of good books." He explains that as we read good books from areas such as "literature, history, exploration, and science and books that tell of the people and places of the earth, your minds will grow and stretch, and you will feel a mental invigoration that will be wonderful to experience."[7]

We are here on earth to learn and grow. Reading enhances our lives as we learn from others' experiences. We gain insight as we learn about other cultures, eras, and ways of life which help us appreciate who we are and to maximize the potential of those things around us. After all, it is knowledge that we take with us when we leave this life.

Journals

We create our own good book when we write in a journal. To write whatever we feel, whenever we want, and to confide these things in our personal journal provides a wonderful companion. These writings become some of our own personal scripture as we discover what does and does not work in our trek called life. Recording these experiences can save us from having to relearn the same lessons.

Writing our experiences helps us remember moments of peace and answers to prayers. "If you desire a further witness, cast your mind upon the night that you cried unto me in your heart, that you might know concerning the truth of these things. Did I not speak peace to your mind concerning the matter? What greater witness can you have than from God" (D&C 6:22–23).

Scripture Reading

President Hinckley also admonished, "Determine now to read the scriptures."[8] As was mentioned in chapter two, it is essential that we read scriptures in our quest to better know and understand the life of Christ and to become more like Him. The scriptures are the text for our class in life.

Paul, observing his son Timothy, said, "And that from a child thou hast known the holy scriptures, which are able to make thee wise unto salvation through faith which is in Christ Jesus. All scripture is given by inspiration of God, and is profitable for doctrine, for reproof, for correction, for instruction in righteousness. That the man of God may be perfect, thoroughly furnished unto all good works" (2 Timothy 3:15–17).

We are admonished to, "Search the scriptures; for they are they which testify of me" (John 5:39). We are also told, "First seek to obtain my word...; study my word which hath gone forth among the children of men" (D&C 11:21–22). "And who so treasureth up my word, shall not be deceived" (Joseph Smith Translation, Matthew 1:37).

Nephi bore testimony of the scriptures: "My soul delighteth

in the scriptures, and my heart pondereth them" (2 Nephi 4:15). We are told through all of our modern day prophets to pray and read scriptures.

It is amazing how often an answer to a problem is revealed as we open the scriptures—sometimes even to the very page. Daily scripture reading also invites the Spirit into our lives and creates a mind-set which helps us act instead of react in difficult situations. President Ezra Taft Benson promised, "There is a power in the [Book of Mormon] which will begin to flow into your lives the moment you begin a serious study of the book. You will find great power to resist temptation…to avoid deception…[and] to stay on the strait and narrow path. The scriptures are called the 'words of life' (see D&C 84:85), and…when you begin to hunger and thirst after those words, you will find life in greater and greater abundance."[9] The scriptures not only help as a roadmap for life but also give us added power and influence when we need it.

Developing Companionship with Your Ward

The church welcomes and includes singles. A good bishop involves his single members even in influential positions of the ward. But some singles find it difficult to be unmarried in a family ward. At one time or another, many of us have felt isolated, different, and conspicuously single. So how do we bite the bullet and make a difference? The following are a few suggestions:

Start by reaching out to others. Yeah, okay, we hear this all the time and you are probably saying, "Why should I be the one doing the reaching?" Remember Lehi's dream when the light illuminated the path before him? Once the path is shown, we must make the effort and go forth.

Many people do not know how to converse with a single member. They feel insecure or uneasy. As we reach out and show them our willingness, others will more likely feel at ease and respond back.

We can see who might need help and offer our companionship by sitting next to them, and make a friend. Initially, we may feel uncomfortable. It may even be difficult, but if we persist, we will break through the barriers and build positive and supportive relationships.

Introducing ourselves to the bishop and offering our services can help. Speaking to single adults, President Hinckley stated, "Men and women such as you have great talents and can add immeasurably to the quality of the teaching and leadership in almost any ward in the Church." It is our responsibility to constantly "remind bishops and other Church officers to give each member a warm welcome and make use of his or her talents." But, he continues, "accept every invitation to serve in the Church. Be true and faithful, be loyal and supportive concerning this glorious work of the Lord."[10]

Fulfilling a calling in the Church is a wonderful way to feel a part of a ward. I know of a ward where single members had callings in the elders quorum presidency, the Relief Society presidency, and the Primary presidency, plus thirty to forty singles from the area participated each Monday with a lesson and volleyball for weekly Family Home Evening. The singles willingly served, got involved, and made a difference not only in each other's lives but also in the lives of ward members.

President Hunter stated, "The Church is for all members...single or married.... The clarion call of the Church is for all to come unto Christ, regardless of their particular circumstances. The Book of Mormon reminds us that the Savior 'inviteth [us] all to come unto him and partake of his goodness, and he denieth none that come unto him, black and white, bond and free, male and female; [and we might parenthetically add single and married]...and all are alike unto God' (2 Nephi 26:33). This is the church of Jesus Christ, not the church of marrieds or singles or any other group or individual. The gospel we preach is the gospel of Jesus Christ, which encompasses all the saving ordinances and covenants necessary to save and exalt every individual who is willing to accept Christ and keep the commandments that He and our Father in Heaven have given."[11]

We can reach a level of understanding our Church leaders share and gain greater confidence as we participate in our ward. Church can then become a place where we look forward to not only reuniting with the Spirit and welcoming its influence but to renewing our commitments with God. With time, we will soften to the environment around us and begin to appreciate and embrace the differences we encounter.

Seek All that Is Good

"We believe in being honest, true, chaste, benevolent, virtuous, and in doing good to all men; if there is anything virtuous, lovely, or of good report or praiseworthy, we seek after these things" (Articles of Faith 1:13). Joseph Smith identifies in the thirteenth Article of Faith what Latter-day Saints ought to seek after. If in the presence of God, would we bring anything less than what is praiseworthy and of good report? Why, as sons and daughters of God, would we allow anything less for ourselves?

President Hinckley said it in another way. "Do you want to eat sawdust when you might have steak? Why waste time on such chaff?"[12] Life is too short to waste time on anything but what is praiseworthy and uplifting. President Hinckley added, "You do not have the time to spend hours and hours listening to and watching that which only degrades and appeals to the animal nature."[13] If that is all we do, that will be all we become.

Good music, uplifting plays, nature, inspiring art of all kinds, and flowers on a day we do not feel so well all add to the quality of life. Let us take the challenge and raise the quality of our lives to a higher, better, and more praiseworthy level.

Cultivate a Companionship with God

President Hunter declared in the April 1994 general conference: "We must know Christ better than we know him; we must remember him more often than we remember him; we must serve him more valiantly than we serve him."[14] What would give more perspective in life and be more fulfilling than to know Christ and God our Eternal Father?

President Hinckley reminded us, "He is your Creator, who loves you. He gave his Son, and his Son gave his life as a sacrifice for you, to open the way that you might gain eternal life."[15]

Nephi shared his testimony of his companionship with God. "My God hath been my support; he hath led me through mine afflictions in the wilderness; and he hath preserved me upon the waters of the great deep. He hath filled me with his love, even unto the consuming of my flesh. He hath confounded mine enemies, unto the causing of them to quake before me. Behold, he hath heard my cry by day, and he hath given me knowledge by visions in the night time. And by day have I waxed bold in mighty prayer before him; yea, my voice have I sent up on high; and angels came down and ministered unto me" (2 Nephi 4:20–25). God will be by our sides if we seek Him and will send ministering angels when we need them. Could there be any greater companionship?

Abigail Morris talks about rebuilding her relationship with Heavenly Father after her engagement breakup. She felt "hurt and abandoned" but her efforts to connect with God up to this point were halfhearted. She admits even her scripture study was halfhearted. However, she explains, "One night, when I felt so miserable I knew I couldn't endure the pain anymore, I poured out my soul in prayer. It didn't start out as a humble prayer. I was hurt, angry, and demanding. But as I felt Heavenly Father's love for me and his concern about my suffering, my heart softened. My petitions became more humble. I acknowledged that he knew what was best. Through the whisperings of the Spirit, he taught me that I needed to learn to forgive before my pain could be healed. He helped me realize that I had been holding on to pain and pride, and that pride can destroy one's sense of self-worth.

"As my prayers became sincere and soul-sustaining, my desire to feast upon the words of Christ grew.... My love for the Savior grew as I read about his visit to the Nephites and about how he bade *each* member of the multitude to 'arise and come forth unto [him]' (3 Nephi 11:14).... But because of his great love for *each* of them, he touched and blessed them one by one. As I read, I felt his love for me, and I wept."[16]

As we listen and follow the inspiration given, we will find ways to overcome and cope with whatever life gives us. There is no one in this world who understands us more than our Father in Heaven. There is no one more interested in hearing, not just what we are thankful for, but what we need. He is our greatest resource and support. There are no greater companions than our Heavenly Father, the Savior, and the Holy Ghost.

Notes

1. Gordon B. Hinckley, *The Wonderful Thing That Is You and the Wonderful Good You Can Do,* 6.

2. Thomas S. Monson, "Formula for Success," *LDS Living,* 21 February 2006.

3. Gordon B. Hinckley, "Women of the Church," *Ensign,* November 1996, 67.

4. Boyd K. Packer, *The Holy Temple*, 38.

5. Ibid., 38–39.

6. Gordon B. Hinckley, "Excerpts from Recent Addresses of President Gordon B. Hinckley," *Ensign*, July 1997, 72–73.

7. *Wonderful Thing*, 7.

8. Ibid.

9. Ezra Taft Benson, "The Book of Mormon—Keystone of Our Religion," *Ensign*, November 1986, 7.

10. Gordon B. Hinckley, "A Conversation with Single Adults," *Liahona*, November 1997, 17.

11. Howard W. Hunter, "The Church Is for All People," *Ensign*, June 1989, 76.

12. *Wonderful Thing*, 7.

13. Ibid.

14. Howard W. Hunter, "'What Manner of Men Ought Ye to Be?'," *Ensign*, May 1994, 64.

15. *Wonderful Thing*, 8.

16. Abigail Morris, "Don't Ask 'What's Wrong with Me?' Find Out 'What's Right with Me'," *Ensign*, March 1989, 36.

Chapter Fourteen

COMING TO TERMS WITH
BEING SINGLE

"LET US FACE THE FACT that in this life some of you will marry, some of you may not. . . . For those who do not marry, this fact of life must be faced squarely. But continuous single status is not without opportunity, without challenge, nor without generous recompense."[1]

Some of us have been single a very long time and others not so long. For some, facing the world single can appear very scary and is "not without challenge," as President Hinckley expressed. However, he also clarified that there are many "opportunities" and room for "generous recompense" in a single's life. As we meet our challenges and change adversity into advantage, every experience can prove to be an opportunity.

Now that is easily said, but how do we change adversity into an advantage? How can we ensure some form of recompense? When the scriptures say, "Men are that they might have joy" (2 Nephi 2:24), does that mean women and singles too? Do we think

193

because of our marital status, it is not okay to be happy? *Are* we happy? What is happiness anyway?

The reality is that many of us drift along hoping happiness and opportunity will find us, unwilling to do what is required to be happy. Although we cannot always control what happens to us—as the sun shines with no effort on our part, so does the rain, sleet, and hail—we can control how we let life affect us. We can create a sense of happiness, even when things are not so good, as President McKay shared:

"Happiness consists not of having, but of being; not of possessing, but of enjoying. It is a warm glow of the heart at peace with itself. A martyr at the stake may have happiness that a king on his throne might envy. Man is the creator of his own happiness. It is the aroma of life, lived in harmony with high ideals. For what a man has he may be dependent upon others; what he is rests with him alone. What he obtains in life is but acquisition; what he attains is true growth."[2]

When we feel a disproportionate share of responsibilities, we know God will prepare a way for us to accomplish those tasks (see 1 Nephi 3:7). We are not alone when we seek His help. He stands at the door and knocks, but it is up to us to open the door and invite Him into our lives.

When we have disappointments and heartaches, never underestimate the value of our present experiences. More importantly, do not give up or give in! Remember these very moments build the foundation for a great and rewarding life, and if we trust God, these experiences will be opportunities for growth and become blessings beyond measure. Peace can be ours—"peace which passeth all understanding."

The question is what can we do on our part to create a sense of peace and happiness even in the midst of life's experiences? Let's read on!

Centeredness

Centeredness is a way to experience peace and happiness in our lives. Centeredness implies we are okay with who and where we are in life, even when the circumstances are not what we had hoped. As in the parable of the wise man who built his house upon rock rather than sand, we stay grounded through the storms because we have a firm spiritual and emotional foundation.

The Tao of Pooh emphasizes the ease with which Winnie the Pooh lives his life; neither questioning life's circumstances nor fretting over what does or does not happen, taking life as it comes. And strangely enough, things work out for him while everyone else experiences anxiety. Pooh is an example of one who trusts the universe, and as a result, a favorable life unfolds for him. We know God is an even greater power than any universe. As we trust Him, we can find this sense of balance and easygoingness as Pooh did, even in the midst of confusion.

I remember learning an important lesson in my life while scuba diving. Eager to get a closer look at some beautiful coral along a reef in Hawaii, I decided to swim toward it. But the more I worked at getting there, the more difficult the struggle of fighting against the current seemed to be.

Tired and worn out, still not reaching the coral, I decided to take a break and relax. To my surprise, the current started carrying me toward the coral. I began to relax when the current went against me and swim when the current went out toward the coral. Amazingly, not only did I get to where I wanted to go, but I got there more quickly and enjoyed the ride much more without the struggle. I was calm, relaxed, and had energy to spare when I reached my destination.

Life is like the ocean. As we try to control such a massive power we will only end up tired, frustrated, and miserable. However, if we point ourselves in the right direction—catch the wave when it comes and not fight the current when against us—we will get to where we are going faster and we will find life's ride more enjoyable.

President Hinckley said, "Life is like an old-time rail journey—delays, sidetracks, smoke, dust, cinders, and jolts interspersed only occasionally by beautiful vistas and thrilling bursts of speed. The trick is to thank the Lord for letting you have the ride."[3]

The brevity of life is real, especially as we grow older and see how quickly time passes. Nothing in this life is certain. What we have today may be gone tomorrow as we can no more control life than we can "add one cubit [to our] stature." Remember the lilies of the field and the fowls of the air? (see Matthew 6:25–30). They do not worry because God takes care of all things.

As long as God is at the center of our universe, we need not worry, even when life does not make sense. It will not matter what we have or do not have because we trust that God will lead us on a path best for us. Should there be someone special in our lives, that indeed is icing on the cake. However, if that person is not present, life is okay because we still have the cake—God. Once we are firm in that relationship, fear transforms into trust.

As the scriptures tell us, seek first the kingdom of God, and all else will be taken care of (see Matthew 6:33).

Coping with Change

One thing consistent about life is that life is not consistent. Change is inevitable. Divorce, death, physical and mental illness, crime, and merely living through life's stages bring some level of change. Becoming single is a tremendous change and often requires redefining one's self as we find new ways to create love, happiness, and fulfillment.

Unfortunately, change is not always easy and finding ways to cope can be difficult. However, to resist change stifles our growth and stagnates our progression. We stay stuck, self-absorbed, and can wallow in self-pity. Self-pity may be okay for a while but at some point, we need to move beyond these feelings in order to serve and love again.

I know a woman whose relationship ended traumatically for her. Twenty years later, although many men had asked her for a date, some even asking her hand in marriage, she remained alone and lonely because she was unable to move beyond her grief.

Studies show those who handle change in a healthy way tend to live longer and happier lives. Of course, we want to live longer and happier lives so how do we handle change in a way that makes our lives more fulfilling?

Loss

In every change there is loss as we let go of one thing to take hold of something new in its place. Even small changes imply loss and can create various feelings and reactions. If we do not acknowledge and grieve the loss, then, when we least expect it, those difficult feelings can surface and affect our behavior. Only through grieving can we begin to look forward and accept a change. This is reminiscent of the title of a seminar I once attended: "We cannot say hello until we say goodbye."

Many of us grieve the loss that accompanies a death, divorce, or faded dreams. Elder Nelson said, "The only way to not feel sorrow at the loss of a loved one is to take love out of life."[4] Who wants to live without love? Who wants to live life without dreaming and hoping? Thus, allowing ourselves to do so means risking loss.

Some think it better to not express emotions related to loss. But the Savior gave us not only an example of compassion but permission to grieve when He "wept" over Lazarus' death (John 11:35). He set a great example—the greatest among us grieving for someone He loved.

Others fear that grieving a loss and letting go of the pain means we no longer care about the person or situation now gone. On the other hand, some believe no matter what they do, the pain will never go away. But not grieving only keeps our focus on the negative and depressive parts of the situation. Grieving allows negative feelings to pass like a breeze or a wind. Soon the burden lifts, and we can take in the wonderful and good parts of the situation. We smile as we remember the warm memories and appreciate the lessons learned.

Captain Moroni queried, "Do ye suppose that the Lord will still deliver us, while we...do not make use of the means which the Lord has provided for us?" (Alma 60:21). Sometimes God lets the natural processes happen so we can expand our experiences here on Earth. We not only learn how to handle emotions in our own lives, but once we experience the healing, we are more able to help others in their recovery efforts. We usually grow the most during our painful moments.

The fact that we live in this human existence means we will experience pain of some kind. Ignoring or fighting against these feelings creates guilt or depression. The energy used to block these difficult feelings holds us back from experiencing life to its fullest.

Because our Father in Heaven loves us, He will not leave us alone. He will walk with us every step of the way. The pain is not easy. Our hurt can feel so deep that it is visceral. However, if we trust our Father in Heaven, He will comfort us, guide us, and teach us. We will experience His healing power, be able to move forward with our lives and ultimately gain what we came here on Earth to learn.

Living in the Present

The Savior said, "Take therefore no thought for tomorrow for the morrow shall take thought for the things of itself" (Matthew

6:34). Confronting His disciples, the Savior said, "Let the dead bury their dead" (Luke 9:60). At another time He declared, "This life is the time for men to prepare to meet God; yea, behold the day of this life is the day for men to perform their labors" (Alma 34:32). The Savior seems to be telling us to let the future take care of the future and the past take care of the past. Our stewardship is now, today, in the present.

Elder Richard L. Evans gave his thoughts on this subject: "It sometimes seems that we live as if we wonder when life is going to begin. It isn't always clear just what we are waiting for, but some of us persist in waiting so long that life skips by—finding us still waiting for something that has been going on all the time.... This is the life in which the work of this life is to be done. Today is as much a part of eternity as any day a thousand years ago or as will be any day a thousand years hence. This is it, whether we are thrilled or disappointed, busy or bored! This is life, and it is passing."[5]

Sometimes we do not want to let go of the past. We wonder what could possibly take its place and end up creating a long list of "If only...." This can create feelings of guilt, failure, being "less than," and depression in the present. Sometimes the familiar, although painful, is more comfortable than facing the unknown. But no matter how wonderful or painful the past, we cannot live it again. Trying to do so only destroys our inner peace.

The future is before us, and however exciting the anticipation or fear, we can only live one day at a time. We will never catch up to the future. To think it possible creates anxiety and keeps us from fully experiencing the present moment.

Thus, living in the past or future contaminates the present with worry and stress. We end up in a perpetual game of waiting or "what-if." This cheats those around us because we limit what we offer others as a part of ourselves is stuck in the past, or worrying or dreaming of the future. We cheat ourselves as well by not living to our fullest.

For example, if we think life will be fine once we are married, what happens if we do not marry? How much time is wasted on waiting and worrying? Learning from the past and allowing the future to give us direction helps us make the most of our situation. However, only by living in the present do we experience peace, calmness, and happiness.

Imagine the Savior coming to visit. How excited we would be to spend time with Him! Imagine that while with us, He was busy planning for the next week's schedule. We would understand, but would there be a little disappointment? Would we feel a little cheated out of what that experience could have been—thinking, *I thought He loved me, but He is too busy planning to spend time with me.* Similarly, those around us may feel the same if we do not give them our time and attention. When we live in the here and now, others feel it, and we all enjoy the moment so much more.

Remain Problem Free

A former BYU bishop once told his single ward members the key to happiness and emotional health as a single person is to remain problem free. Resolving problems as they arise keeps past problems from influencing our present lives.

If we carry our "emotional baggage" from the past into the present, we set ourselves up for disaster. Imagine a man not only carrying a piece of luggage in each hand but also bags under each arm, a huge trunk on his back, and perhaps a chain of suitcases tied to his feet—lugging and dragging all of this along as he walks!

Discarding our emotional garbage—even those deep-seated issues, wounds, or traumas from both childhood and adulthood—is vital. Only then will we have room to let in what is good. How do we dump the garbage? Follow the Spirit. God will lead us toward emotional health and, if needed, to those who can help in the healing process.

The nice thing about the present is that we can change any behaviors we no longer want. As we shape each moment for the better, those moments build into days, the days into weeks, weeks into months, and then years. In the end, we find a life full of growth and positive change. We will find there is little time to worry about the past or the future.

Try This Exercise

To help keep in touch with the present, take a deep breath and hold it for ten seconds. Now, slowly exhale through your mouth, again to the count of ten. Do this three times, slowly. Next, close your eyes. What do you hear, smell, feel? Finally, open your eyes. What do you see?

As you engage each sense, register how each one feels. Contentment and joy come from the fragrance of a small wild flower, warmth of a spring day, beauty of a bird in flight, the comforting sound of water rippling along in a brook. We notice the fluffy clouds in the sky or the baby's cry—the big and magnificent to the very simple and small things, even down to the veins on a leaf—each can bring us joy.

Now remove yourself from any other outside noises or disturbance such as the radio or TV, and begin clearing the noise within. Quietly listen and enjoy the silence. This is sometimes difficult due to a fear of what we may discover in the process of getting through all the noise in our heads. It may take awhile, but as we quiet our minds, sit still, and listen, we will discover wonderful treasures within us. Our Father in Heaven has told us, "be still, and know that I am God" (Psalm 46:10). With time, we will feel His Spirit. He will instruct and comfort us, and in so doing, we will find we are much more present in the moment.

Another way to focus on the present is to ask, "How would I live this day if it were my last?" If we lived each day as if it were our last, we would live every day to its fullest. We would appreciate the things that matter. We would hear music as if for the first time. We would see friends with "new eyes" as if we had not seen them for a long time. We would share time, talents, and ourselves like we have never done before. Moreover, we would take time to find those things that fulfill us, and we would give as much as we could to the world around us.

Other questions to ask are, "When I look back on life, will I feel like something was missing? Will I regret not giving, loving, and serving more? Will I feel despair at not living life to its fullest, or will I feel a sense of peace knowing I did all I could?" Putting all of our heart, soul, and mind into each moment helps us make the most of the time in our lives. Taking advantage of opportunity and creating memories not only enriches our lives but creates a sense of fulfillment.

When we experience pain, we need only remind ourselves that "this too shall pass." The pain may not feel good in the moment, but we can recognize that even pain is a friend as it teaches us the value of joy and happiness and helps us appreciate more fully what is good in life. Pain teaches us empathy and allows us to grow and become a better person. We can reach a level of comfort and share our understanding and support with those who battle the same kinds of pain. As a result, we develop Christlike character.

One of the most powerful ways to make the most of the present is to daily renew our relationship with our Father in Heaven and feed our spiritual selves. As we connect with our Father in Heaven in daily prayer, we will be more aware of His love for us, and, hence, our faith will grow and we will have greater strength to follow His will.

As we follow the Savior's lead, He will carry us through difficult times. He will wash away our sins and help remove what stands in the way of our relationship with God.

As we develop our ability to hear more clearly the still, small voice of the Spirit and more diligently follow those promptings, we will reach our highest potential—be it a quiet hero behind the scene or on the front lines of the battle.

Making the Most of Life

"I suppose if I have learned anything in life, it is that we are to keep moving, keep trying—as long as we breathe! If we do, we will be surprised at how much more can still be done."[6] President Kimball summarized his thoughts with his motto: just "Do it!"

Charlotte did not start out with any extras. She came from an alcoholic family in poor circumstances, had been abused, and had little money, but did not let that hold her back. Charlotte gave 110 percent. Determined to be a lifeguard, Charlotte became one. Wanting to be a good tennis player—though an easy fifty pounds overweight—she made the local college tennis team. Deciding to sing and play the guitar, Charlotte did just that—not always singing on key, but anyone listening knew she enjoyed herself!

Perhaps one of the greatest challenges was her determination to graduate from college. If tested for learning disabilities, she probably would have had some, for college courses were difficult for her. It was painful watching her struggle through assignments; still every assignment was completed and turned in. Charlotte's grades were not the highest and she took twice as long as most to complete her education.

Nevertheless, working to pay her own way through school, and older than most of the other students, Charlotte graduated with a degree in elementary education. Well-known as a teacher of sixth-graders competing to be in her class for fifteen years, Charlotte never saw limits. She never told herself or her students that they could not "do it." They went ahead and "did it" anyway, together!

Although Charlotte never married, perhaps her greatest contribution included her efforts to fulfill her patriarchal blessing that said she would some day have children. She grew outside of herself into motherhood when she became a single foster mother. Her foster child, Kari, was included in all of Charlotte's activities—biking, hiking, camping, and canoeing. In three short years, this little ten-year-old girl developed from being a troubled child into a person with self-esteem, good grades, and excellence in sports. Charlotte made a significant contribution.

When Charlotte died unexpectedly, hundreds of people traveled near and far to pay their respects at her funeral. No one mentioned the kind of car she drove, the size of the house she owned, or the money Charlotte had in the bank. No one mentioned her travels or what brands of clothing she had in her closet. What was mentioned were her character, her talents, her contributions made to others, and how Charlotte never limited herself even when the experts would have told her to do so. What is Charlotte's legacy? It is her determination, laughter, and desire to enjoy life. She fought the good fight and our Father in Heaven must be pleased.

"Men should be anxiously engaged in a good cause, and do many things of their own free will, and bring to pass much righteousness; for the power is in them" (D&C 58:27–28). Charlotte made the most of her forty-five years of life in spite of the limitations she inherited. Our challenge is to have the courage to move beyond our limitations, hold nothing back, and offer life our very best—to fill each moment to the fullest.

Developing Gratitude

When upon life's billows you are tempest-tossed,
When you are discouraged, thinking all is lost,

Count your many blessings; name them one by one,
And it will surprise you what the Lord has done.

Are you ever burdened with a load of care?
Does the cross seem heavy you are called to bear?
Count your many blessings; every doubt will fly,
And you will be singing as the days go by.

Count your blessings; Name them one by one.
Count your blessings; See what God hath done.
Count your blessings; Name them one by one.
Count your many blessings; See what God hath done.

So amid the conflict, whether great or small,
Do not be discouraged; God is over all.
Count your many blessings; angels will attend,
Help and comfort give you to your journey's end.[7]

Whenever you feel lonely, depressed or think that life is unfair, begin a blessing list as this song suggests. Initially you may get stuck and wonder what to be thankful for. You may need time to really think hard. But as you begin such a list you will be amazed at what happens. You will recognize the positives in your life, and suddenly what seemed so heavy and burdensome becomes light.

We can complain about our pain and loneliness, and become self-centered. However, regardless of our marital status, everyone struggles with some level of loneliness and pain. President Hinckley reminded singles, "You think that this [marriage] would be the answer to all your problems. While a happy marriage should be the goal of every normal Latter-day Saint, let me assure you that for many who are married, life is miserable and filled with fears and anxiety....

"I say that only to remind you that there are those who are married whose lives are extremely unhappy and that you who are single and experience much of deep and consuming worry are not alone in your feelings."[8]

In the book *A Singular Life*, Mary Ellen Edmunds explains her "theory of relativity" when talking about gratitude. She tells that while serving a health mission in Indonesia in 1977, one of the missionaries received a newspaper clipping reporting that California was experiencing a drought, and that people had to cut back to 120 gallons of water per person per day. Sister Edmunds tells of her observation of the local people who walked to a nearby well to dip their buckets and carry their daily supply of water to their small dirt floor houses. She wondered what it would be like if each person in that little town of Jakarta had 120 gallons of water to use each day!

That February, the Church asked for a special fast for those suffering from the drought in the western United States. Sister Edmunds expressed amazement when observing how many of the members in Jakarta who only ate one meal a day—not because of fasting but because they did not have the food—faithfully fasted. She recalls that one local brother prayed, "And please, Heavenly Father, take care of those who are suffering because they don't have enough water. We have plenty. Could you take some of ours and share it with them?"

Sister Edmunds summarizes her perspective with this: "I know there will always be many people who have much, much more than I do—more time, more clothes, more talent, more hair, more pets, more toys, more children, more things—but there will also always be millions who have much, much less than I do, and in many situations much, much less than they need. I began to understand it is not *what I have*, but *what I enjoy* that brings real happiness."[9]

Gratitude is a characteristic of true inner nobility. We focus on our blessings, strengths, and talents, rather than on our shortcomings and problems. Then to show our gratefulness, we share those positives with the world around us.

I think of an early morning walk years ago with a friend, a young mother of four, married three times, and the third marriage ending. She was upset and felt like a failure. To keep perspective, I asked "Which situation would you rather be in, married three times, all ending in divorce, but having your four beautiful children, or never marrying, like me, and never having children?" Without hesitation, her response indicated her decisive assurance to be in her situation and have her children.

Although we may not see fairness in this life, we can be assured our Heavenly Father will make sure all is fair in the eternities. Everyone will be blessed, and all will be whole if we trust Him and follow His lead.

Ten lepers came to Jesus seeking healing. All were healed. Only one returned to give thanks. Jesus said, "Were there not ten cleansed? but where *are* the nine? There are not found that returned to give glory to God, save this stranger. And he said unto him, Arise, go thy way: thy faith hath made thee whole" (Luke 17:17–19). As we continually remember to thank our Father in Heaven for what He has given us, our gratitude and faith will help make us whole.

Live with an Eternal Perspective

President Spencer W. Kimball once said, "If we looked at mortality as the whole of existence, then pain, sorrow, failure, and short life would be calamity. But if we look upon life as an eternal thing stretching far into the premortal past and on into the eternal post death future, then, all happenings may be put in proper perspective."[10]

We could easily conclude that life is not fair and become bitter, angry, and discouraged. This would be a shortsighted view. But, as

Paul explained to the Corinthians, "For now we see through a glass darkly; but then face to face; now I know in part; but then shall I know even as also I am known" (1 Corinthians 13:12). Even if we do not now fully understand and sometimes are confused, we will one day comprehend it all. We just need to remember to "be of good cheer, and not fear, for [the Lord is] with [us], and will stand by [us]" (D&C 68:6)—at all times, no matter our present situation, as long as we are obedient to what we know it right.

President Hunter addressing singles, said, "The promises of the prophets of God have always been that the Lord is mindful of you; if you are faithful, *all* blessings will be yours. To be without marriage and a family in this life is but a temporary condition, and eternity is a long time. President Benson reminded us that 'time is numbered only to man. God has your eternal perspective in mind.' (*Ensign,* Nov. 1988, p. 97.)"[11]

We may never reach complete peace with our singleness, although that is available to us if we seek it, but we must come to terms with it and live by faith if we want to reach our potential and accomplish what we were sent to earth to do.

Charles Steizle said, "If you sit still long enough, you'll never get up again. If you never lift your arm, you'll soon be unable to raise it at all. If you remain in darkness and never use your eyes, you'll soon become blind.... The process of disintegration and death begins when a man shuts himself out from the forces that make for life."[12]

Some of us do shut ourselves off from the forces of life, God. We determine our life isn't important enough, we are not good enough or, out of self-pity or depression, we just sit still and do not move. Like the servant in the parable who lost even the talent given him by his master because he failed to use and prosper with it, we regress and lessen in our own ability to do that which we can to help those around us (Matthew 25:14–29).

Arnold Bennett commented, "The real tragedy is the tragedy of the man [or woman] who never in his life braces himself for his one supreme effort, who never stretches to his full capacity, never stands up to his full stature."[13]

Many of us live in a trance, half awake, in a manner far less than the one meant for us. Moroni uses the words "awake, and arise" (Moroni 10:31), and Nephi writes, "Awake, my soul!" (2 Nephi 4:28). Perhaps they were admonishing that we move beyond ourselves and stop searching for what life might offer. Rather, we are better served if we seek to know what we can offer life. Perhaps they would encourage us to find our purpose in life, right here and now.

Will we regret not having offered or given more, not having lived and grown more before moving on to our third estate? Ask: "What difference in this world can I make with the time, talents, and means with which God has blessed me? What is my purpose?" By doing this and following the path identified we will begin living our lives more "awake," and in line with our potential.

In fact, some of the most influential people in history were single. They obviously rose above the loneliness, the self-centeredness, and self-limitations and made a difference in the world. Joan of Arc forever changed English and French history. Florence Nightingale impacted hundreds of ill military personnel. Mother Teresa dedicated her life to relieving suffering in the world. President Lee, President Hunter and President Hinckley were single for extended periods during their presidencies of the church and continued moving the church forward without missing a step.

So how did they rise above it all? How did they get the energy, vision, courage, and inspiration to move ahead with their lives when others might have sat back waiting for something to happen?

Look to God

Some may say, but "I want my needs met before I go out to meet the needs of others. I need my cup filled first." The reality is that we all need to fall on our knees and bring our Father in Heaven and the Savior into our lives before we move forward. Only through our relationship with our Heavenly Father and His Son, Jesus Christ, will we feel the deep, abiding love and companionship we long for. This is how our "cup is filled." Once filled with His love we are then ready to become instruments in God's hands. Only then are we given the love and knowledge of how to lift others.

By giving our lives over to God, we develop the understanding of our purpose here on earth, thus receiving the extra boost we need to magnify our talents and the energy to contribute what we were sent here to offer. Only then do we stop the search for that part of us that remains unfilled because we are now fulfilled with God, the Savior, and the Holy Ghost in our lives.

I suggest it is summed up in a scripture in Alma 37:47. "Look to God and live." Could anything be more profound, more inspiring, more to the point than this simple phrase? Perhaps "live" in this scripture implies more than just existing. Perhaps "live" could be considered the ultimate action word, getting up and doing, putting forth effort and energy into our existence, putting our all into life. "Looking to God" implies that He is our focus, our lead. When we "Look to God and live" could life be any more fulfilling or more purposeful?

> Waiting at the checkout stand, Jenny saw them: a circle of glistening white pearls in a pink foil box. "Oh please, Mommy. Can I have them? Please, Mommy, please!" Quickly the mother checked the back of the little foil box and then looked back into the pleading blue eyes of her little girl's upturned face. "A dollar ninety-five. That's almost $2.00. If you really want them,

I'll think of some extra chores for you and in no time you can save enough money to buy them for yourself. Your birthday's only a week away and you might get another crisp dollar bill from Grandma."

As soon as Jenny got home, she emptied her penny bank and counted out 17 pennies. After dinner, she did more than her share of chores and she went to the neighbor and asked Mrs. McJames if she could pick dandelions for ten cents. On her birthday, Grandma did give her another new dollar bill and at last she had enough money to buy the necklace.

Jenny loved her pearls. They made her feel dressed up and grown up. She wore them everywhere; Sunday school, kindergarten, even to bed. The only time she took them off was when she went swimming or had a bubble bath. Mother said if they got wet, they might turn her neck green.

Jenny had a very loving daddy and every night when she was ready for bed, he would stop whatever he was doing and come upstairs to read her a story. One night when he finished the story, he asked Jenny, "Do you love me?"

"Oh yes, Daddy, You know that I love you."

"Then give me your pearls."

"Oh Daddy, not my pearls, But you can have Princess the white horse from my collection. The one with the pink tail. Remember, Daddy? The one you gave me. She's my favorite."

"That's okay, Honey. Daddy loves you. Good night." And he brushed her cheek with a kiss.

About a week later, after the story time, Jenny's daddy asked again, "Do you love me?"

"Daddy, you know I love you."

"Then will you give me your pearls?"

"Oh Daddy, not my pearls, But you can have my baby doll. The brand new one I got for my birthday. She is so beautiful and you can have the yellow blanket that matches her sleeper."

"That's okay. Sleep well. God bless you, little one. Daddy loves you." And as always, he brushed her cheek with a gentle kiss.

A few nights later when her daddy came in, Jenny was sitting on her bed with her legs crossed Indian style. As he came close, he noticed her chin was trembling and one silent tear rolled down her cheek. "What is it, Jenny? What's the matter?" Jenny didn't say anything, but lifted her little hand up to her daddy. And when she opened it, there was her little pearl necklace. With a little quiver, she finally said, "Here, Daddy. It's for you."

With tears gathering in his own eyes, Jenny's kind daddy reached out with one hand to take the dime-store necklace, and with the other hand he reached into his pocket and pulled out a blue velvet case with a small strand of beautiful genuine pearls and gave them to Jenny. He had had them all the time. He was just waiting for her to give up the dime-store stuff so he could give her the genuine treasure.[14]

Great joy awaits those who willingly give themselves and that which they possess over to God. What we receive in return is far greater and of much more value than what we could ever create on our own. He gives us what is real, genuine, and what really matters. He, through the atonement of His Son, completes us and makes us whole.

Today is a glorious time to live, even if we do not have everything we had hoped for. We have a great opportunity to serve, give, and create a life full of love and memories that brings joy not only to others, but will be pleasing for us to look back on, single or not. As we align our lives with the blueprints created specifically for us, we will find peace, energy, and a sense of purpose and value. Life will unfold and we will fulfill the measure of our creation.

Above all, our relationship with God is what matters. Are we making the most of the time allotted us in this life? Do we make a difference in the world? Are we growing to our greatest potential? Will God say to us, "Well done thou good and faithful servant" (Matthew 25:21)? He will if we turn our lives over to Him and follow the Spirit's promptings.

No matter where we are in our "climb up the mountain of life," we can always begin anew. We can start right where we are. You see, it is not so important where we are along the way as long as we are going the right direction and following our Heavenly Father's will. The Lord promises us, "I will go before your face. I will be on your right hand and on your left, and my Spirit shall be in your hearts, and mine angels round about you, to bear you up" (D&C 84:88).

Moroni's farewell to those whom he loved sums it up. "And now, I would commend you to seek this Jesus of whom the prophets and apostles have written, that the grace of God the Father, and also the Lord Jesus Christ, and the Holy Ghost, which beareth record of them, may be and abide in you forever. Amen" (Ether 12:41).

My wish for all of us is to "seek this Jesus" who loves us, to develop a personal relationship with our Father in Heaven through prayer, and to learn to hear and follow the sacred guidance and direction of the Holy Spirit. As we rid ourselves of those things that stand in the way of these relationships, we will be given new life that is whole, complete, and filled with joy and peace. The reality is, though single, we are *never alone.*

Notes

1. Gordon B. Hinckley, "A Conversation with Single Adults," *Liahona*, November 1997, 17.

2. David O. McKay, *Pathways to Happiness,* comp. Llewelyn R. McKay (1961), 104.

3. Gordon B. Hinckley, *Cornerstones of a Happy Home,* (pamphlet, from broadcast, 29 January 1984).

4. Russell M. Nelson, "Doors of Death," *Ensign,* May 1992.

5. Richard L. Evans, *Improvement Era,* January 1967, 65.

6. Spencer W. Kimball, "'Do Not Weary by the Way,'" *Ensign,* November 1980, 76.

7. "Count Your Blessings," *Hymns,* no. 241.

8. Gordon B. Hinckley, "A Conversation with Single Adults," *Liahona,* Nov. 1997, 17.

9. Mary Ellen Edmunds, *A Singular Life,* 141, 143–144.

10. Spencer W. Kimball, *Faith Precedes the Miracle,* 97.

11. Howard W. Hunter, "The Church Is for All People," *Ensign,* June 1989, 75.

12. Charles Steizle, *Utah Labor News,* 12 December 1937.

13. Spencer W. Kimball, *The Miracle of Forgiveness,* 94.

14. "Beautiful Pearls," as shared with the author by Susie Martin, E-mail, June 15, 1999.

APPENDIX

Continued discussion on building great companionships in our lives—healthy dating relationships and positive potential partners.

Healthy Dating Relationships

SOME OF THE MOST UN-CHRISTLIKE BEHAVIOR happens when we date. Respect for one another as a son or daughter of God is often forgotten when, more times than not, our focus is on ourselves and what we can get out of the dating relationship.

Entering relationships with self-centeredness and selfish motives, we run the risk of disrespect and misuse of the other person. Being insensitive to each other's feelings, we can damage self-esteem. Defenses build up, anger develops, and a fear to enter into other relationships is often the outcome. A bishop at BYU counseled his single ward members to have a temple worthy influence on those they date. In other words, he wanted them to make sure that the persons they date would be more worthy to attend the temple as a result of their time together. Unfortunately, this does not always happen.

Asking ourselves, "What can I offer the relationship?" versus, "What can I get out of the relationship" shifts our thinking from selfishly taking to sharing. If we focus on Christ-centered dating and consider "What would Jesus do?" both individuals end up contributing to the growth and life of the other.

You see, in Christ-centered dating, when we truly love, that love stays, no matter what happens to the relationship. There are no strings attached. "I love you because I do." We are kind and gentle. We give and extend ourselves, but, most importantly, we are respectful because we recognize each other's divine heritage. We care about our partners physically, emotionally, and spiritually, and, because of the time spent together, that relationship becomes valuable, even if the dating part of the relationship ends.

In Christ-centered dating, we respect the other person. We honor their decisions and the paths they choose even if they do not include us.

Christ-centered dating is built on truth. For example, one partner may stay in a relationship so as not to hurt the other or one may use the other for selfish purposes. In either case, the individuals have not been honest. In the end, someone gets hurt and a price is paid for making choices outside of truth.

In Christ-centered dating we can trust our attraction one toward another. Maybe there is a quality or characteristic from which we can grow or something we can give.

In Christ-centered dating, we are more resilient and can more easily work through our pain to stay open and trusting. The fact is we are all imperfect beings living in an imperfect world. Disappointment and hurt occur. If we follow the Savior's lead, the lessons we learn will leave us wiser and better individuals.

In Christ-centered dating, we find our associations more fulfilling. We end up grateful for the time together and for the opportunity to love and grow.

Positive Potential Partners

Someone once said, "Choose carefully whom you love, then love the one you choose." Unfortunately, some of us do not take the time or ask the questions that help to ensure a secure and loving marriage relationship. For example, some fall in love with a fantasy and when the partner ends up not matching the dream, many discard the partner. These people then search for a person to match their ideal, but because the image is not realistic, they never find the perfect person and often find themselves alone.

Some become social workers in their private lives and are convinced that if they love and care enough for another, that person will change. These people can spend many disappointing years in a relationship—a marriage—and become disillusioned when the partner does not change.

Some are determined to marry only an exemplary leader or the rose already in bloom. They forget that no one grows to greatness without starting out as a bud. A loving and healthy relationship is the water and sunshine that help a bud, or person, blossom. Sister Kimball once said, "When people ask what it feels like to be married to a prophet, I tell them, 'I didn't marry a prophet. I married a young returned missionary.'"[1]

When we seek perfection in a partner, it means we have not found perfection or wholeness in ourselves. In other words, we project what is missing in ourselves onto another. So, as soon as we start pointing a finger, complaining about what is missing in another, it is time to see what is missing in ourselves.

When choosing a marriage partner, there are three important questions to answer:

1. Do I love this person?
2. Is this relationship healthy?

3. Do I have confirmation from the Spirit that this relationship is right for me?

As we seek the answers to these questions—being honest in our hearts with a clear "yes" to all three—we will find greater success in our eternal marriage relationships.

A good question to ask in measuring our level of love is, "Would we be willing to stay with this person if they got in an accident and became totally disabled?" That decision would not mean in an enabling or care-taking way but to truly love this person no matter what happens to them. Rob demonstrates genuine love as he continues to love and sacrifice for his wife even after an accident that left her paralyzed from her neck down. Though she cannot function normally and the load is tremendous on him, it is not even a question for him as to what to do. He remains committed and continues to demonstrate genuine caring and love despite the circumstances.

How do we know if a relationship is healthy? Some fall in love only to find out later how unhealthy the relationship really is. For example, Cary fell in love with a man who ended up emotionally abusing her. Because of her love for him, she continued to stay in the relationship far beyond what was healthy. She lost self-esteem, self-confidence, and, now separated, lives in fear of being stalked.

A healthy couple requires health in each partner. This means we do our work within and become a healthy individual first. This takes effort which is sometimes painful. However, as mentioned earlier, when we bring God into our lives, because He is perfect and whole, He will help fill the gaps. He may also require that we take steps on our own to complete the work. The Spirit will direct us as to where and to whom we go or open a path for us to mend—be it emotionally, socially, or physically.

We can also determine our own level of self-esteem and emotional health by looking at those with whom we associate, as we often spend time with those whose character and sense of worth match our own. Looking at our companionships can be quite revealing. If we are not happy with what we see, we can ask for the Spirit to guide us toward the path and the people that will influence us in a more positive way.

The third question to ask is, "Does God approve of the relationship?" We need to be somewhat careful about this because a relationship may be a right dating association but not the individual for marriage. In other words, this person may be in our lives for a particular reason at this time to help in a particular way.

If we are sincere in our hearts as we ask whether someone is in our lives temporarily or could be our eternal mate, we will recognize the confirmation we receive. As we place God at the center of our relationships, one of three things will happen.

1. If the relationship is not healthy, the Spirit will let us know. If we will listen, it will direct us away from negative influences.

2. If the relationship is healthy and the Spirit confirms the association, but does not confirm that this person should be our eternal mate, we can rest assured that there is a purpose and a reason for the relationship. In seeing the relationship through to its natural ending and trusting God, we will grow and blossom in ways our Father in Heaven intended.

3. If we receive and recognize the confirmation that the person we are dating is "the one" to marry, then, despite our fear, we will have the confidence to follow through.

As we focus on keeping God at the center of every association, we will find depth and meaning in each experience, and trust that every connection will be for good.

Notes

1. Edward L. Kimball, ed., *The writings of Camilla Eyring Kimball,* (1988).

Single,
Yet 🐾 Not
Alone

A Spiritual Guide for Latter-day Saint Singles

www.singleyetnotalone.com

QUICK ORDER FORM

Fax: (916) 241-9906 **Telephone:** (916) 903-7299
Mail: Anela Press, P.O. Box 1585, Fair Oaks, CA 95628 USA
Web site: www.singleyetnotalone.com

Please send ____ copies of Single, Yet Not Alone @ $15.95 ea _____
Tax for books shipped to California addresses (7.75%) @ $1.23 ea _____

US Shipping and handling

Media mail (average 9–15 days), first book $3.80 _____
For each additional book, add $1.80 _____
Or
Priority mail (average 3–5 days), first book $6.80 _____
For each additional book, add $2.80 _____

International shipping

First book $11.00 _____
Each additional book, add $5.00 _____

TOTAL $ _____

PAYMENT ENCLOSED

☐ Check   ☐ Credit card
☐ Visa   ☐ Master Card
Card Number _____
Expiration date _____ (mm/yyyy)

In case of problem with order

Phone (_____) _____

E-mail address _____

PLEASE SHIP TO

Name _____

Address _____

City _____ State _____ Zip _____

Single,
Yet ⚜ Not
Alone

A Spiritual Guide for Latter-day Saint Singles

www.singleyetnotalone.com

QUICK ORDER FORM

Fax: (916) 241-9906 **Telephone:** (916) 903-7299
Mail: Anela Press, P.O. Box 1585, Fair Oaks, CA 95628 USA
Web site: www.singleyetnotalone.com

Please send ____ copies of Single, Yet Not Alone @ $15.95 ea   _____

Tax for books shipped to California addresses (7.75%) @ $1.23 ea   _____

US Shipping and handling

Media mail (average 9–15 days), first book $3.80   _____

For each additional book, add $1.80   _____

Or

Priority mail (average 3–5 days), first book $6.80   _____

For each additional book, add $2.80   _____

International shipping

First book $11.00   _____

Each additional book, add $5.00   _____

TOTAL $ _____

PAYMENT ENCLOSED

☐ Check   ☐ Credit card

☐ Visa   ☐ Master Card

Card Number _____

Expiration date_____ (mm/yyyy)

In case of problem with order

Phone (_____) _____

E-mail address _____

PLEASE SHIP TO

Name _____

Address _____

City _____ State _____ Zip _____